METHOD-OR MADNESS?

Mr. Lewis lecturing on *Method—or Madness?* Playhouse Theatre, New York.

METHOD-OR MADNESS?

By Robert Lewis

WITH AN INTRODUCTION BY HAROLD CLURMAN

SAMUEL FRENCH, INC.

NEW YORK   TORONTO   HOLLYWOOD

The excerpts from the Craig-Stanislavski conversations are reprinted by permission of Eugene Ilyin and Plays and Players Magazine, London.

The selections from *Building a Character* by Constantin Stanislavski are reprinted by permission of Theatre Arts Books, New York, Copyright 1949 by Elizabeth Reynolds Hapgood for Stanislavski's heirs.

ISBN 0573 69033 2

CONTENTS

ILLUSTRATIONS

These informal lectures delivered by Robert Lewis to an audience of professional actors constitute a kind of codicil to the classics of the subject, the three books by Constantin Stanislavski, "father" of the so-called (Stanislavski) "method" or, as its originator himself called it, "system." References to, and quotations from, these three books are amply and effectively made in these lectures.

The distinguishing feature of the Lewis lectures, beside their humor, is their *common sense*. As I read these lectures, I recalled a maxim I once heard, the author of which I no longer remember: "Better a good doctor with the wrong theory, than a bad one with the right theory." Though Lewis is a good "doctor" with the right theory, the maxim might well have been the motto of his lectures.

Common sense has become rather desperately needed in regard to the Method which may simply be defined as a codified formalization of the technique of acting.

The reason why so much nonsense and amateur gibberish is bandied about apropos of this reasoned and reasonable subject is an abiding appetite among us for "magic."

We are always in search of something that is novel and that works like a charm. One swallow of this new medicine three times a day—after shaking the student well—and "hey, presto!" you have a marvellous actor, an artist, perhaps even a genius.

The reader may have noticed that I called the Method a formalization of *the technique of acting.* I did not say "realistic" acting. The distinction is important because the Method was introduced to Stanislavski's (Moscow Art) theatre around 1911 in the heyday of the realistic play: Chekhov, Gorki, *et al,* and to the American theatre between 1925–35 when plays by Sidney Kingsley, Clifford Odets and kindred playwrights were attracting special attention. It was in such plays that the efficacy of the Method was strikingly demonstrated. My point is that though there is an historical or chronological correspondence between the realistic school of dramaturgy and the Method, the Method relates to *every kind of acting*—good acting—and not narrowly to realistic acting as such.

It cannot be emphasized too much that the Method is not a style. Style in the theatre depends on the nature of the play presented, the production ideas and temperament of the director and the performing company. The Method *is* technique, a method for the training of the actor so that with experience over the years he may develop a technique for the most complete use of himself as an interpreter of parts in plays.

That what I am saying is a fact and not merely my own view of the matter is exemplified by Lewis' own work as a practicing—and successful—director on Broadway. Himself trained as an actor in the Method—in the Group

Theatre which in America first applied the Method in production on a broad scale—Lewis has directed, among other plays, Saroyan's *My Heart's in the Highlands,* a poetic play, *Brigadoon,* a musical, *The Happy Time,* a comedy of French Canadian manners and *The Teahouse of the August Moon,* which, though somewhat stylized in production, is a traditionally American type of comedy.

Here then is theatre talk from a showman, talk which clears the air of the hothouse fumes that have gathered around the sensible structure of the Method—useful and needed talk.

New York City, July 15, 1958

APRIL 15, 1957

BACKGROUND

FIRST LECTURE: *Background*

TIME: *April 15, 1957. 11:30 P.M.*
SCENE: *The auditorium and bare stage of the Playhouse Theatre in New York City. The house is humming with over 700 actors, some playwrights, designers, and a few drama critics. On stage is a high stool, a lectern and a table. From left comes the Lecturer, staggering under the weight of his documented evidence: books by and about Stanislavski, huge volumes on techniques of theatre and other arts, magazines, and even a precious, ancient phonograph recording of Tommaso Salvini. The applause greeting the speaker is augmented by laughter as he carefully unloads his props onto the table and faces his theatre colleagues.*

I really ought to stop while I'm ahead.
Well, here we go. Or perhaps I should say—here we go

again. Because I've been hearing so darned much talk on the pros and cons of the "Method" I thought I'd give eight more lectures on it! Not that I simply want to add more talking: it's just that so much of the talk has been so confusing that it was beginning to confuse me. Maybe, together, we can clear up a few points here.

For example, I've been hearing, "The Method is the only answer to truthful acting." Yet I know of great actors who are completely unaware of it: and I know of other great actors who *are* aware of it and violently opposed to it. Then again I hear, "The Method is a curse, it is ruining the theatre." Yet I know of great actors who, I feel, are doing nothing that is incompatible with what I understand the Method to be. I hear, further, that the Method is limiting—useful only in "family plays about the Bronx;" that it is useless for Shakespeare and frowned upon by good English actors.

> [*Here I left the tall stool I used as a perch and, crossing to the table, picked up a volume:* THE ACTOR'S WAYS AND MEANS *by Michael Redgrave.*]

And yet, there is a great and continuing tribute paid to it in this book by a famous English Shakespearean actor. Yes, everything is documented tonight!

A great deal of the time one hears that Method actors are "mumblers." When a producer friend of mine heard I was going to talk on this subject, he had just one thing to say: "When people pay $5.50, they have a right to hear what's being said!"

Yet the actor who was one of the most important inspirations for Stanislavski in the early period when he was for-

4

mulating his Method was Tommaso Salvini, the famous Italian actor. And he's the fellow who said, "The three requisites to play a great tragic rôle are voice, voice—and more voice." George Henry Lewes, the eminent English critic, who saw Salvini toward the end of his career in *Othello*, said that in certain scenes he felt Salvini was the greatest speaker he had ever heard. Parenthetically, it is interesting, knowing Stanislavski's love of truth, that Lewes also said that Salvini "overacted and underfelt." However, we weren't there and it is awfully hard to check reports on past performances. I do have, though, a phonograph record of Salvini's voice. I don't have the equipment here to play it but, at least for evidence, I'll show it to you. There! (*Here I held it up.*) I tell you this whole thing's documented like the F.B.I. tonight! This is, I believe, the only existing record of Tommaso Salvini in this country—at least, it'd better be—I paid the guy enough for it. I got it from a record collector in a very small town in England. It's a Zonophone Disc, made in Milan, about 1903 I imagine. *Il Sogno di Saul* (The Dream of Saul) is the name of the piece, from the play, *Saul*, by Alfieri, who is considered by many to be the Italian Shakespeare. Now, Salvini was born in 1829. So he was pretty old when this was made. But, even at that, this record is definite proof that Salvini was a very great "speaker." Stanislavski, in other words, did not go to hear a mumbler and decide to formulate a system for mumbling—that came much later!

Stanislavski says here, in his book, *Building a Character,* "I recall, for instance, the soliloquy of Corrado in the melodrama, *Family of a Criminal,* as played by Tommaso Salvini. This soliloquy described a criminal's escape from prison. I was ignorant of the Italian language: I had no idea what the actor was narrating, but I was deeply involved in all the detailed emotions he was experiencing. I was helped to this, largely, not only by the magnificent intonations of Salvini, but also by the remarkably clear-cut expressive tempo-rhythm of his speech."

Now, in a way, conflicting opinion is very natural in an art, as there are no absolute answers. It should be fun to have these arguments and be on one side or another. But I find that on this particular subject, the Method, the talk is often very bitter and personal—not properly polemical as it should be. One hears, for example, rumors of producers and directors who are reported to employ only "Method actors," and of other producers and directors who will not touch a "Method actor" with a ten-foot contract. Now, on this platform, I would like to try to lift the discussion, if possible, onto a more technical plane with a cool examination of the subject. Of course, before I finish I may get killed in the crossfire!

Now, I personally read every letter of application for admission to this series, some five thousand of them, because I was interested in knowing what you felt, what you wanted to hear, and what you thought I was going to say. A large number of the letters defended the Method and a large number of them blasted it. A large number forgot to enclose the requested stamped envelope to receive the admission ticket!

From studying the letters it seemed to me that there are four categories of opinion extant on the Method. First, there are the "True Believers." These are the insular ones. They feel part of a holy order, and all outsiders are infidels.

The second group we'll call the "Angry Knockers." These often know nothing about it at all but somehow feel left out of something. Then there's the very large third group —the "Giddy Misconceivers." They possibly attended one class, held by a friend of a former student of someone who was thrown out of an early 1930 class given in the summer by Mme. Ouspenskaya! I also sensed a small but determined fourth group (they mostly just said, "Send me a ticket.") who seemed objectively interested in all theatre techniques. I would like to enlarge this group.

And now to get down to business. I will attempt first of all to describe what I think the Method is. I will try, at least, to lift the veil of what some people feel is secrecy. Why they feel it's a secret I'll never know; (*holding up Stanislavski's two books*) there's the bible, *An Actor Prepares* and *Building a Character*. They have only to read the two volumes; everything's in there; and there are loads of other books on the subject. The feeling of secrecy may come from two sources. First, it may come from the sort of High-Priest attitude of some of the "propagators of the faith." And secondly, from a kind of "professional" fear of anything that has a scholarly tinge to it. Why this fear should exist in some actors I don't know, since performing dancers, singers, violinists—especially great ones—study and practice all their lives; and the finer their equipment the more technique they need to support it.

I will try to point out what I feel are the uses of the Method and its possible misinterpretations. Perhaps by talking it over with you I can help to clarify some points for myself, too. At the end of every season of teaching in my workshop I always found that if nothing else had happened, a lot of things were cleared up for me. After all, as a stage director I am faced with these pros and cons in rehearsal all the time. As in my workshop, what I seek here is illumination—not "the ultimate answer." There are no boundaries in art. I don't want to make more, but less, dogma here. Dogma may be all right in some quarters, but it doesn't agree very well with artists. When I used to lecture at the Yale School of the Drama I always tried to remember to say at the beginning of each term that I would consider my best pupil to be the one who would listen most carefully to what I said and then most gracefully forget the whole thing! I hope you will do that too, because I feel that an artist's study goes into his being and then comes out some way, unconsciously, in his work.

I now would like to give you an outline of the points I am going to cover in these eight talks, so that you get a sense of the whole. First, I'm going to try to trace my own personal history with the Method, which spans over some twenty-eight years. I do not pose as an expert on the Method—I just feel that after brushing with it for over a quarter of a century something should have rubbed off by now. Then I will try to trace for you the history of the Method itself. After that, I will discuss acting techniques in general. You know there is more than one method! Further, I will try to define the Method and describe it in detail from the authentic writings and diagrams of the originator himself, and, after that, try to point out what I feel are its uses and misuses. Then I will come to a not-too-original question: What is truth? Of course I mean what is truth in acting? That will probably be a hot session because I think there are more artistic crimes committed in the

8

name of truth than in the name of any other virtue. *Whose* truth? What can be more phony than some "truth" we see parading our boards? Is the purpose of the Method to create *real everyday life* on the stage—and who wants it? Next: Actor or artist? Does the manner in which various practitioners work on the Method aim too often at training certain limited specific elements of acting rather than at developing good artists? In this section I will also discuss acting as it relates to music, painting and other arts. Finally, the Method in connection with poetic theatre, musicals, Shakespeare, etc.

Now about my history with the Method: The first time I remember ever hearing anything that sounded like it was in 1929. I was an acting apprentice in Eva LeGallienne's Civic Repertory Company. A rehearsal was going on—it may have been *Romeo and Juliet* or one of the other plays in which I had a small part—and Miss LeGallienne and Mr. Jacob Ben-Ami were having a discussion on the stage. I can't remember what he said, but I remember her replying, "Oh, that's what they call 'emotional memory,' isn't it?" It meant nothing to me at the time. Later I realized that what they were referring to was a Stanislavski term which, in the Group Theatre days, we called "affective memory." I will attempt to define this specifically for you bye-and-bye. But let me tell you first of my earliest observation of the application of one aspect of the Stanislavski approach in performance.

Jacob Ben-Ami was in the Civic Repertory Company in 1929. He was a wonderful actor, and still is—a lyrical actor, with genuine feeling and high imagination. I gravitated toward him more than toward the other actors, and sort of apprenticed myself to him. There was something about his acting that intrigued me, and so I helped him in ways that would keep me near him while he worked. I held his script for him while he studied his lines, and cued him. Incidentally, I remember his once saying something which would probably shock some holier-than-thou modern Method disciples. I was cueing him while he was going over his lines in *The Cherry Orchard* when I heard him say, "Now let me see—I say, 'Something in the nature of a cockroach' . . . then the audience laughs . . . and then I say . . ."

At any rate, one of the plays we did was *The Living Corpse,* by Tolstoi. I was a waiter in a scene with Ben-Ami. I had to open a champagne bottle—pull the cork out and make it pop. It's not easy. In any event, shortly after I went off the stage, he had a great moment. I want to tell you about it because it was one of the first times in my life that something happened on a stage which was memorable enough to stay with me my whole life. Our theatre lives are made up of these great moments, and I used to watch this one every night from the wings. *Fedya* was the character Ben-Ami played in *The Living Corpse* and the moment came when he had to attempt suicide. He wanted to free his wife from their marriage and so he wrote a farewell note (that's what he was doing when I was trying to get that champagne bottle open!), took a gun and tried to kill himself. But he couldn't—he didn't have the courage. Now, earlier that season, I had seen the Reinhardt Players do the same play. The man who played *Fedya* was their great actor, Alexander Moissi. He had made an enormous success in the part, and this same moment was unforgettable in his performance, too. If any of you here remember it, you will know what I mean. I won't try to imitate either Moissi or Ben-Ami, but just for purposes of demonstration I would like at least to try to describe to you the difference in what happened at this moment in each portrayal.

Moissi, as you know, had a beautiful voice. He sang well —I heard him sing—and there are many recordings of his speaking voice. Now I remember this particular moment in the Reinhardt production of *The Living Corpse* when Moissi put the gun to his head, [*here I demonstrated*] held it there for a second, and then let out this piercing wail, "*Ich kann nicht!*" Then the next second somebody banged on the door and Moissi whispered, excitedly, something like "Who's there? Just a minute!" The great change from this terrific cry to that whispering was so shocking, dynamically, that it was unforgettable: a magnificent moment. Ben-Ami in that same moment in the play was quite different. He went to a mirror, looked into it, started to bring the gun up to his forehead, and as he got about here, almost to it [*here I was demonstrating again*], the audience let out a gasp, every single time! *They thought he was going to do it.* Then he said, brokenly, "I can't . . . I can't . . ." and put the gun away.

In the first case, Moissi's was a world-famous effect. You could read about it in the "Who's Who" in the back of the program! When it told about his career it said that he was famous for this moment; so you looked for it, like you wait for the shooting of the apple in *William Tell*. But the reason I speak about its being so "effective" is that the same moment, although executed quite differently, was

11

also highly effective in the case of Jacob Ben-Ami. The audience never gasped in Moissi's case as they did in Ben-Ami's. Try to follow me through this because it leads to my ultimate points. The effect that Moissi made was stunningly "theatrical." It was a real physical thrill. I remember it clearly. I can even hear the sound in my ear to this day. The effect that Ben-Ami made with different means was, I maintain, *theatrical* too. But it was not only physically exciting; there was an internal thrill to it as well, which moves me to this very day when I think about it. Now both actors had good "meaning;" it wasn't that one was "mechanical" with no "inner content," and the other full of "psychology," but no "form." They both had the general idea of the terror of committing suicide. Moissi's performance of the inability of a weak man to go through with it was theatrically superb. However, in the Ben-Ami realization you were specifically worried for *Fedya*. You felt, in Ben-Ami's case, that he was a failure even at suicide, where the other fellow, as one thinks back on it now, was quite brilliant at not killing himself!

Now I got up my courage after a while to ask Ben-Ami how he invariably made the audience react the way they did in that moment; what went through him that made it so real to them that they gasped and really thought he was going to do it. He wouldn't tell me for a long time. Finally he explained, "Well, you'll laugh, but I'll tell you. I didn't know how to do it when I first came to rehearse it because —well, let's face it, I've never committed suicide! So I said to myself, 'What must shooting yourself be *like?* Perhaps I can *imagine* something about it.' Well, I thought to myself, just *one* of the things that must be true about putting

12

a bullet through your head is that it must hurt a lot! You must think it's going to hurt a lot, anyway, and you're probably afraid of that. So there is that fear of the *physical* pain; that much at least must be in it, outside of everything else. Now what fear do I have of some physical shock or pain? And here's where you're going to laugh. Because I wanted it to be a kind of growing fear as I got closer and closer to my forehead with the gun, I suddenly thought that when I turn on a cold shower and have to propel myself into that cold water—well, the physical terror of how that's going to feel when it hits is pretty strong with me! Also, it is a sensation I can easily recreate; it is close to me—I do it often. Now," he said, "the truly created sensation of the imminent shock of the cold shower, if they can believe I am really terrified of this thing, *plus* the appearance of the gun in my hand—the real thing right there in front of them—will make them imagine it is really happening." The combination of the two things really worked. The audience gasped every time that gun got up there.

Later on, when I thought back on this explanation, I realized the importance of Ben-Ami's "opening that door" for me in 1929 which led me to the 1931–41 decade of the Group Theatre and even up to tonight's search. I was to ask myself over and over whether, in the desire to create truth on the stage, one need sacrifice a sense of the theatrical. Whether, to achieve theatricality, one had to toss overboard the elements of real truth. Whether truly-experienced acting on the stage couldn't be, and shouldn't be, exciting; yes, and even poetic. Moissi's brilliant effect had been achieved with exciting physical means. Ben-

13

Ami's moment had been compounded of imagination and personally experienced sensations, and still was highly theatrical.

Now about the tradition of the Method itself. We ought to know something about that. Because just as technique should be an unconscious guide in any specific work that we do, tradition should be the unconscious guide in our general creative outlook. Of course, one of the bad aspects of tradition is that the original ideas of an innovator get sifted through his followers and often run the danger of being diluted, or even warped. The good aspect of tradition is the fact that it is the way in which ideas are handed down to us.

There are many examples of tradition in the performing arts. For example, here's a little book [*Here I lifted a large volume full of the most beautiful pages of musical exercises*] which is called, *The Art of Song*. It's a *method* of singing. This is a modern binding I had put on it for protection because the book is over a hundred years old. Anyway, it's the Garcia method of singing. Manuel Garcia was born in 1775, in Seville, Spain. He taught his daughter, Pauline Viardot, to sing with his method. She was born in Paris. Pauline Viardot taught Félia Litvinne the Garcia method of singing. Litvinne was born in St. Petersburg. Félia Litvinne taught Nina Koshetz to sing. She was born in Kiev. Nina Koshetz came to America and taught the same Garcia method to an American girl, Marion Bell, who sang the leading role in *Brigadoon*, which I directed.

Now the Stanislavski method dates from the end of the last century when Salvini and other great acting stars visited Russia. Stanislavski had been bothered about his

14

acting; he felt something was wrong, unsatisfactory. He studied these great actors and attempted to put down what he learned from them. He had a studio in which he tried to work out these ideas; you would recognize the names of some of the members of that studio—one of them became a famous motion picture director, Richard Boleslavski, and there were others. Boleslavski had a studio here in this country which was called the American Laboratory Theatre. There went people like Lee Strasberg, Stella Adler and other names that you would know. Then, in the early thirties, some of these people, and others, started the Group Theatre. That theatre went on for ten years and its actors studied with Strasberg and Harold Clurman. Those actors developed into teachers who then formed a studio and taught other actors. In that studio Sanford Meisner, Elia Kazan and I taught. Then in 1947—we've come half a century already—Kazan, Cheryl Crawford and I started the Actors' Studio which still operates. I was there just the first year and after that I went out and formed my own private workshop. In that first year at the Actors' Studio my class included Montgomery Clift, Marlon Brando, David Wayne, Jerome Robbins, Tom Ewell, Eli Wallach, John Forsythe, Karl Malden, Herbert Berghof, Mildred Dunnock, Maureen Stapleton, to name just a few. Today Herbert Berghof, and others of that group, teach, and I understand that some of *their* pupils are now teaching also. And so it goes on.

Now then, what is technique? Well, I looked it up in Webster's Dictionary. It says, "An expert *method* in execution of the technical details of accomplishing something, especially in the creative arts, as the technique of a master violinist, etc." Now if "method" has become a confusing word to you, you could, if you wish, use the word "technique." Also, while some berate Method practitioners, I think few will admit that they themselves have no technique. Ah, yes—but *what* technique? Well, now there are some formalized techniques; and then there are the "do-it-yourself" varieties. I'll give you first some examples of formalized techniques. Remember, I said there was more than one.

Some of you probably have heard of the "Epic" theory of acting of the German playwright and director, Bertolt Brecht. This is the theory which purports to *set the action of a play before you* rather than *involve* you in it by means of empathy. This technique of "distancing" the action is called *"verfremdung."* That's all I'm going to tell you about it—we're mixed up enough already! However, Brecht's company has only recently made a wonderfully interesting impression, using the theories of Mr. Brecht, in their season in London.

Then there is a system of acting called "Bio-mechanics," which has no relation to realistic acting at all. It was developed by a Moscow Art Theatre rebel named Meyerhold and is subordinated entirely to mechanics and mathematics. One aspect of this theory is based on a series of work movements, for example. It is called "Taylorism" and is like the system of the Ford assembly line: one person does a movement to accomplish part of a task, then another picks it up from there, etc. Movement based on this system led Meyerhold to a needed style. Well, I'm not going to tell you anything more about that in these lectures, either. I just want to point out that there are many methods. We must presume, however, that what is meant by "The Method" as it is being discussed around Downey's [Note: *An actor's restaurant on Eighth Ave. in N.Y.C.*] is the system set down by Constantin Stanislavski, or, more probably, some derivative of that system.

Now, as to the do-it-yourself breed. It is true that there are, and have been in the past, some fortunate wonders with little technical knowledge of any kind who can create, and have created, artistically, by instinct alone. They represent a form of genius. Sometimes we call them "naturals." Then there are those a little less gifted, who can achieve this result intermittently. Now the purpose of a technique is to stimulate this creative process when you need it. I'll change that to *as* you need it, and I will leave it to your artistic consciences if you don't feel that we mortals need that stimulus from time to time.

Most actors have some technique—some method. I have found in my directing that the majority of the *self-appointed* "naturals" who profess no knowledge of any known technique, have an extensive one all their own. Most of them plead, "I don't know what I do. I just go out onstage and something happens; some fog of inspiration descends on me and I *am* the rôle!" Well, the fog part is quite true. What do they do, I often wonder, when that inspiration isn't there? Fake it, I guess. (I once directed an actor who was like that—a foggy one—and he used, occasionally, to give some sloppy performances. He was a very good actor, by the way; he just didn't know what he was doing. The play, unfortunately, was a hit, so the number of "off" performances piled up. I would go to him and we'd review all of the points in his part and, for a bit, all would go well. Then, chaos again. So it would go on until finally one day he said, "Look, it's a long run, and I just *have* to give one bad performance a week." Well, that was the one he *knew* of!)

Now I have found that a lot of these "naturals" have the most extensive technique for *effects*, if not for stirring up their creative juices; they plan every look, every gesture, every inflection—but purely mechanically. And they have a jargon that makes the Method terms seem like child's play. They say, "Feed me. Lay it in to me." They want to make an effect by having their cues given to them loudly, so that they can reply softly, or given to them softly, so that they can reply loudly. They also have stage movements worked out, either for self-aggrandizement or public modesty. They'll say, "Let *him* stand up center there and say that one line; I could step down here and give him the stage." What they usually mean when they say they're going to step down and give the center to him on that one line is that they are going to take it all the rest of the time. Oh, they have a lot of tricks!

So actually it comes down to the fact that there are two kinds of technique: There is the one that devotes itself to interpretation, and there is the other that devotes itself to self-exploitation. That does not mean that the first need be, or should be, "psychological" (almost used as a synonym for "introverted" in theatre discussions these days); and that the second is "theatrical," and "you takes your choice." When Bernard Shaw wrote his famous essay about Duse and Bernhardt, which I am not going to read—one always reads it at a time like this, but I assume you've all read it in his *Dramatic Opinions and Essays*—I feel he did not mean that Bernhardt was beautiful, charming and *theatrical,* and that Duse was old, drab and *naturalistic* (like "life" as they say!). I think he simply felt that Duse used her great beauty, charm, and sense of theatre to enact a character and nail the theme of the play to the stage, instead of for self-aggrandizement. This is one answer to those who are forever inferring that theatricality is necessarily phony, or that truth need be drab.

Now a word about the purpose of technique. Technique is a guide; it is there if, when, and as, you need it. If a painter wants a certain specific color, his technique helps him to mix that color; then he's off again, painting. When a composer needs a difficult modulation from one key to another, his technical knowledge of key relationships helps him make that modulation. However, if he is not a painter or a composer in the first place, technical knowledge alone will not make him one. There is no guarantee that if you do everything right, according to *any* method, the result will be acceptable art. There are some untalented technical experts in acting, as well as some very talented actors who cannot execute the simplest technical problems.

Technique is a means—not an end in itself. For example, when a good dancer is performing on the stage, his daily, laborious, technical, bar-work is forgotten in his desire to express some *idea in movement.* If, during a turn, or in a leap, he said to himself, "Now here is where I'm going to shift my balance" instead of "knowing it" in his body, he might just break a leg for his pains! Yet, how many times do we actors "break our legs," psychologically speaking, by *playing our technique* rather than the scene. Martha Graham, one of our greatest performing artists, says that

19

the aim of techniques is "to free the spirit"—that's her way of putting it. Notice that she says, "free the spirit," not "bind the body!" You know what I mean if you've seen some actors with their technique showing, as I have. Graham has a dance, I can't think of the name of it at the moment, some sort of pavane, as I remember—where she puts both her hands and both her elbows onto the floor and slowly lifts her whole body up to a precarious angle, with feet high in the air. It is a truly great *technical* feat, but she doesn't do it for that reason at all. It's done for an idea, the idea, possibly, that the court is standing on its head and everything is upside down. Then, too, her costume is made of stiff material, not for any personal reason of appearance or comfort, but for an idea—the idea of encasement, perhaps. These are the artist's uses of technical knowledge. Degas, the painter, said that if you own 100,-000 francs' worth of craftsmanship, spend five sous to buy more. Now this doesn't mean you have to stick to all the rules in art in any limiting way at all. The rules can all be broken; but it is wise at least to know *what* you're breaking. So much for technique in a general sense.

Good night. See you next week.

APRIL 22, 1957

THE METHOD ITSELF

As I said last week, we have to assume that what is meant by "The Method" is the Stanislavski System, or some derivative of it. Tonight I am going to try to tell you the elements that make up the Stanislavski system. Although I have studied the system and read most of the books on it over the years, my most direct connection with the words of the Master himself came in 1934. I was an actor in the Group Theatre at the time. Two members of that theatre, Stella Adler and Harold Clurman, went to Paris, where Stanislavski was recuperating from an illness, and spent several weeks with him that year. While there Miss Adler copied out a complete chart of the various elements of his system. The material of this chart was discussed in detail in his books, *An Actor Prepares,* and *Building a Character,* when they were published later, the first in 1936, and the second in 1949. I don't believe the fascinating chart itself was ever published. [*See Illustration.*]

Now I want to tell you right off that I worry about this cursory examination of the Method I am going to have to make tonight. It is dangerous, in one short evening, even to try to summarize the work that a great theatrical master spent a lifetime on. It is, however, the only way that I can try to define correctly for you his terms that one continuously hears bandied about; also, it is the only way I can point out to you the presence of certain elements which I feel are not emphasized strongly enough or are totally neglected by various exponents of the Method. I know that I run the risk of confusing some of you who have had no contact at all with the Method. I've thought it over very carefully, several times resolving to skip this evening entirely, and I've decided it is the only way to keep what I'm going to say in all these eight talks from once again becoming general or, worse, mysterious. The thought that finally determined me was, "Well, it's all published anyway, and there's nothing I'm going to say that isn't in the two books." At least in this way I can have an opportunity to take the elements apart a little for you. I will read you the chart and try to define, as completely as possible, each term.

Before I start I would like to ask you please to remember this: I am not teaching the Method here by doing this—it cannot be done that way. I am simply going to read the chart and try to explain the content for you as I understand it for the purpose of making my points later on. I don't want anyone hearing these talks to go out and say they studied the Method with Bobby Lewis. And what's worse, then go and open a school! That sort of thing has been done, you know. Now you can *describe* dance movement, for example, on a lecture platform—you cannot teach it very well from there. To teach it you should have the pupil right with you. You have to show him how it's done. He has to try it and you have to tell him when he's got it, and so on. It's quite a different process from hearing a lecture about it. In teaching you deal with the actual materials, not ideas alone. I do not want to add one bit to the pile of hash that is built up by the inept teaching that goes on in all the performing arts.

Ahhh—now here is the chart; this is my original copy. [*Here I held it up.*] I've had it since 1934. It's so worn; look, you can see the holes in it. I scotch-taped it this morning so it would last through this evening. I feel like Sophie Tucker showing her original copy of "Some Of These Days." The only difference is that I always felt she makes a new one each year. This is my original—it really is; see, there is the date in the corner—1934.

Now this chart looks forbidding. As a matter of fact, this lecture will be the most technical of all. Once this is over, we can get back again to the fun of loose opinion! At any rate, this is simply an attempt to put down in some organized form what good actors are doing when they are acting well. You may say, "That's an impossible task in a performing art; how can you codify it?" Well, Garcia did it with that vocal method I showed you in that wonderful big book last week. It was all down there, his whole technique. Laban in Germany, and others all over the world, have worked for years, and are, in fact, still working on a dance notation with which they record ballet performances, etc. They don't say if you follow that notation you'll be a dancer. What is put down are the steps; they still have to be danced. It is a means to an end.

Well, let's tackle the Stanislavski chart. As you see, it's

in the form of a pipe organ. Straight across the bottom, number One, is the sort of great foot pedal which says, "Work on one's self." This pedal supports the whole edifice. Above this basic one, there are four other pedals, numbers Two, Three, Four and Five. Number Two says, "Action;" Three—"Truth of feeling or passion (the resemblance to Truth under the given circumstances)." Four—"The creation of life, nature, or true feeling, with the help of conscious technique (beats) which arouses the subconscious;" Five—"The creation on the stage of the life of our Soul (this is the purpose of our art—not the life of the body—the body is just the instrument)." Six and Seven are divided equally across the page: Six says, "The process of feeling (internally);" Seven—"The process of expressing your emotion." Eight, Nine and Ten, equally divided into three parts, are what he called "The three motors of our psychic life: The three musicians who play the organ pipes 11–40. They are Mind, Will and Emotion." Mind is the least capricious; Will is less capricious; and Emotion is the most capricious. Getting frightened?

Now come the various pipes, from Eleven to Forty. Eleven to Twenty-seven all deal with the process of feeling, internally. (By the way, some of these terms are a little outdated now. This chart dates from 1934. You'll find, in *An Actor Prepares,* for example, that "Action" is called "Objective," etc.) Eleven is "Action itself;" Twelve—"Magic If;" Thirteen—"Given circumstances;" Fourteen—"Beats;" Fifteen—"Problems (the choice of little actions, or activities);" Sixteen—"Imagination;" Seventeen—"Emotional memory;" Eighteen—"Attention (to the object);" Nineteen—"Feeling of truth, the belief in what you do;"

Twenty—"The exchange of sentiments (speaking to the eyes);" Twenty-one—"To recreate emotion to show different colors;" Twenty-two—"The fluid of exchange of emotion;" Twenty-three—"The control that removes clichés (the judge of yourself);" Twenty-four—"The finishing of problems (beats), and mastery in movement." Being on this side of the chart, this means *inner* movement. Twenty-five—"Theatrical personality and scenic sympathy (taking away the bad things that make bad personalities);" Twenty-six—"Ethical discipline (props, makeup, quarrels, etc.);" Twenty-seven—"Tempo-rhythm."

Now, Twenty-eight to Forty represent the process of expressing your emotion (this will come as a shock to those "Psychology-only" Stanislavski-ites). Twenty-eight—"Relaxation;" Twenty-nine—"External tempo and rhythm;" Thirty—"Placement of voice;" Thirty-one—"Diction (the feeling of the soul of the language by knowing the nature of sounds);" Thirty-two—"Rules of speaking: 1. Intonation, 2. Pauses, 3. Accent (to do design and get things from comma);" Thirty-three—"The sentiments of the language;" Thirty-four—"Movement;" Thirty-five—"Dancing;" Thirty-six—"Fencing;" Thirty-seven—"Sports;" Thirty-eight—"Acrobatics;" Thirty-nine—"Plastique;" Forty—"The way of walking."

Across the top Stanislavski has drawn a line with a letter "A" encompassing the whole process which on this chart is called "the Transaction" and which, when accomplished, equals "B," called here the "Spine" (in *An Actor Prepares*, the Super-objective).

Now, all of these pipes on the left, 11–27, represent the complete internal, inner feeling—letter "C." The right side, 28–40, leading up to the letter "D," is the complete external. These two, joined together, are "E," which equals "the Part." That's the chart as I received it in 1934.

Now for a bit of elucidation of the terms. Take number One first: "Work on one's self." Well, we're probably doing that right now. I think Stanislavski does not mean so much work on the artist's character alone, because that is only part of it. We know people with fairly poor characters who are fine actors, and we know people of splendid character who can't act at all. But I think what he probably means is that when you are expressing yourself in a part, somehow all your reactions to life, all the ideas and feelings that you have stored up, come out in one way or another. Therefore, you should work to enlarge your knowledge of the world, the people in it, and their characters and relationships. Also, you should sharpen your observance of situations in life, develop your imagination and sensitivity, because those are the things which you store up to feed you in whatever you do in your work. The process goes on all the time with all artists, but one should make a continuing effort in that direction. It is so basic that it is put down as the foundation of the whole edifice.

Numbers Two through Five are four basic pedals, or principles of the Method, which reappear in more detailed form in the pipes (11–40), so I will leave their definitions till later. Number Six, the pedal which supports the entire left half of the organ means that this fifty per cent of the Method is devoted to all the internal problems of acting, emotional and psychological. It is in this area that most of the discussion of the Method usually lies. But right opposite, is Number Seven, which underlines all the processes of "Expressing your Emotion," a subject more likely to be sniffed at by the Devoted. And yet, there it is, fifty per cent worth!

Eight, Nine and Ten, "the three motors of our Psychic life," as they are rather floridly called here, are Mind, Will and Feeling (Emotion). The first gives us the ideas and the understanding, the second gives us the power to execute our wishes, or problems, and the third fills us with the fuel of expression. The Mind is the easiest to control, says Stanislavski, the Will a little harder, and needs disciplining, and Emotion is the hardest of all to summon and control. For all these problems he has exercises, but here we are only going as far as defining. The études you can read about in his books, and in any case, they come clear in classroom work only, as I have indicated.

We come now to number Eleven. This word "Action" as used here in 1934 was the term we employed in the Group Theatre, too. (Of course it meant *inner* action— not physical action.) If you have read the books, you know it is translated by Mrs. Hapgood as "Objective." (The "Spine" is called the "Super-objective.") These days some refer to "Action" as "Intention." It has been called many things in many books and some people don't call it anything; but it is a process that is going on, if they are really acting. I myself don't care if you call it spinach, if you know what it is, and do it, because it is one of the most important elements in acting. Good actors who never heard of, or care nothing about, the Method, are conscious of the importance of this part of their work. Now I'd like to tell you what it is.

Action (or Intention) means what really is happening on the stage, regardless of what you are saying. It is, in a sense, your reason for being in the scene. We know that in a play, especially a good play, as in life, one does not always mean exactly what one says. Of course it is perfectly possible that you *can* mean exactly what you say: one character may say to another, "I love you," and that may be exactly what is meant and all that is meant: that *I*, this man, *love you*, this girl. It is explicit in the line and that is what is intended to be conveyed. But it is also possible that something quite different is intended by those words. You might hear one character *sneer* the words, "I love you." It's perfectly clear that he is trying to let the other one know that he *despises* her, yet he's using the very same words. His *intention*, therefore is quite different this time. In the first instance he wished to convey his deep affection for this girl; with the second approach he wished to let that person know he despised her. The reading of the words, "I love you," is only part of acting; it is *what you wish to convey* with those words that is important. Now this process of intention goes on not only when you are speaking; it is present all the time, whether you are speaking, listening, or standing alone on the stage, thinking. It is a continuing component of acting which is very basic. It is, in a way, even more important than emotion. Actors often think that feeling is everything. But it is quite possible, if you are continually expressing your correct intention in every scene, to carry on the sense of the play for an entire evening with very little feeling. If you violate this principle, however, it doesn't matter how much feeling you have, or how fine an effect you make, you are

30

simply not conveying the intention of the scenes, and therefore you are doing violence to the play.

For example: you may have to say to somebody in a play, "I *knew* you did it!" And your intention is *to let that person know you suspected him all along.* Now you can convey that idea with more or less feeling, but you must always convey that idea. That is, in fact, the "story point," as the writer would say. You can murmur, "I knew you did it!" with little feeling; or, if at that moment you have been worked up to a certain point and you have more emotion, you can explode, "I KNEW YOU DID IT!" [*Here I illustrated the two examples.*] In each case, however, you must get over the idea that you always suspected him. But, if you come out on the stage and say [*and here I illustrated the vague, secretive, mumbling, halting style of so many successful pseudo "realists" today*], "I nooya . . . ya . . . ya . . . ya . . . didut!" you may very well make a wonderful impression for your repressed excitability, you may very well feel fine yourself, you may very well prove you can make a lot of interesting, although irrelevant, movements, you may get over the idea that where the author had written one "you," you said four, and you may even make some people feel that, having changed the word "you" to "ya," you are more sexy; *but,* you have not solved the problem of that moment in the play. You have not solved it because you have given the impression that you have just at that moment been surprised with the information, which is not the point of the scene. The point is *to let the fellow know you always suspected him;* not that you've just found out about it and are indeed surprised to find out about it. More plays go

31

down the drain in this way than the stunned authors or the highly-praised actors suspect.

By the "Magic If," number Twelve, I presume is meant the simple phrase, "it is as if," that is always in the consciousness of good actors, and, in fact, good artists in any field. There are things you may not have actually experienced, but you work *as if* you have experienced them. I gave a very basic example of that last week when I talked about Mr. Ben-Ami. Although he had no actual knowledge of what it felt like to put a bullet through his head, he said to himself, "What *would* it be like? What would the *nature* of it be? Well, it would be *as if*—" and he was off to the races. As a director I constantly hear myself saying to actors, "Do it *as if* you have said it to him for the tenth time." "Talk to your husband in this scene *as if* you're talking to a child." The "Magic If" is the springboard of our imagination, one of our most powerful weapons.

Thirteen—"Given circumstances." Well that sounds pretty forbidding. Actually it's a term that was also used by Pushkin. In reply to an inquiry from an author, Pushkin wrote, "The truth of passion, the verisimilitude of feeling, placed in the given circumstances, that is what our reason demands of a writer or of a dramatic poet." It means, for the actor, the circumstances that have taken place that may affect your scene. Let's take *Hamlet:* the circumstances that exist before *Hamlet's* part begins are that his father, whom he adored, has died and his mother has married *Hamlet's* uncle shortly thereafter. In his first scene he sets about finding out something about those given circumstances. Besides the circumstances that are "given" before a play starts, there are circumstances in the very scenes

32

you are playing either "given" by the situation, or created by the actor or director to enhance the playing. The "circumstances," for example, of a taxi waiting for you outside, with meter ticking, might well hasten your pace in your on-stage scene. Instead of standing around in rehearsal moaning, "I don't feel it," when the director requires a certain result for the scene, the actor might often profitably create some "circumstance" within the logic of the situation to permit him to execute what's required.

"Beats"—Number Fourteen—what that means, quite simply, is the distance from the beginning to the end of an intention. Your wish "to let him know you always suspected him" (your intention) might start with the line, "I knew you did it," and continue through for the next six lines of your part. It might last for just that one line and then change. It might continue for a whole scene; you might have nothing else to do in the scene but that—to let him know you always suspected him. But the distance from the beginning to the end of an intention is called the "beat." It corresponds roughly to phrases in music. We will see later how you can mark the "sides" of your part with your "intentions," etc., and so create a "score" for yourself.

Fifteen—"Problems." Those are what we might call the "little intentions" that go to make up the large one. For example: suppose I was going to "stick-up" a party and I had to come into the room where the party was going on "to case the joint." That is my main intention in the scene. First, when the butler opens the door, I study him and the way he takes my hat and I figure it's a pretty rich apartment; this is part one in my "casing the joint." Next,

I look into the room, checking over the furnishings and observing what kind of people are there. That's the next little "problem" I have within the main intention. Then I see the hostess and I study her from a distance—and her necklace. (I make up very corny plays.) Anyway, the point is that my main desire "to case the joint" is fulfilled by the successful execution of these various small "problems."

(I must stop for a moment to remind you that I'm not *teaching* this here in this way. I'm just trying to describe what is meant by these terms because I will need to refer to them later when I discuss the uses and misuses of the Method. I am merely *defining* now, and quickly, at that.)

Sixteen—"Imagination." Stanislavski knew this to be a thoroughly practical piece of technical equipment for the actor. He put it down here big as life as one of the most important ingredients of acting. He actually has, in his book, suggestions as to how one can develop the imagination, as well as exercises for this purpose. He doesn't say he can give an imagination to somebody who doesn't have it. I don't suppose one would be a very good actor anyway if one didn't have an imagination. But, he says, one can develop the imagination—one can work on it. After all, it is something that is used in a practical way on the stage all the time. Nothing is real up there. That girl isn't your sister —she's an actress; that painting is not really a Picasso— it's something the designer and the prop man put together, etc., etc. You are using your imagination all the time on the stage, not only about physical things, but about ideas too. One must be able to imagine situations and believe in them. Imagination is an important and practical tool of the actor.

"Emotional memory"—Number Seventeen. I wish I could be a coward and skip over this one entirely. Because it is something one should discuss and work on in a small class and much less publicly than this. This is the same item that was subsequently referred to as *"affective memory"* in the Group Theatre days. Now, normally, it is something which every fine actor has at his beck and call always. Ellen Terry tells, in her Memoirs, of helping herself emotionally on the stage by recalling music heard in the great Normandy churches she had visited. An actor worth his salt has stored up within himself memories of all sorts of experiences and feelings. When coming up against a situation in a play requiring a certain emotion, he can evoke the memory of some similar emotion in his life without his thinking consciously about it at all. The greatest actors do that. It is the grist for the mill of the creative artist. A writer, painter, or composer is fed by this all the time. But an actor has to appear on the stage himself and at a specific time has to feel a certain way. Very often that little old emotion just doesn't come when needed, especially if it's a deep feeling not easily provoked by the goings-on of the moment. Stanislavski thought there might be a way in which it could be summoned in these special cases. He worked out an exercise for it that can be used for this purpose.

The theory is that if, quietly relaxed, you think back over a certain incident in your life which moved you strongly at the time, and if you can remember and recreate in your mind the physical circumstances of that moment (where you were, who was there, what happened, the time of day, the place, surroundings) and start reliving it—not trying to remember how you *felt,* a lot of people make that mistake—it is possible that a feeling similar to what you felt at that time will recur. If it was a very strong emotion and you can bring it back successfully three times in a row, it is quite possible you have something that will work for you for a long time. The exercise gets simpler as you do it over and again; and, finally, you only need think of some aspect of it and it's probable your feeling will come back. For those of you who have never done anything like this, it all may seem very dubious, but it is possible. We know this process occurs often in life. You're telling someone about something that happened and suddenly you start to be moved again by the experience. Stanislavski tried to work this out so that it can be used as material by the creative actor. Of course a great deal of the nonsense that used to be spoken about the Group Theatre in the thirties came from this particular item. It's dangerous territory to tread, in any case.

Eighteen—"Attention." In his book, Stanislavski calls it "Concentration of Attention" or, more simply, Concentration. It means the same thing—the attention you put on a specific object. It doesn't mean just the general concentration you should have in your work; it goes without saying that every good performing artist has to concentrate on what he is doing. Stanislavski doesn't mean that. He means to be able, by your *choice,* and with your *will,* to focus your attention wherever you wish; it is that which helps determine the importance of what is happening in a scene. For example, I (in the character of a lecturer) am here putting my concentration at this moment on describing and defining, as best I can, the terms in the Stanislavski method to you, the audience. Various other things are occupying me too (the microphone here, recording my voice, that I must talk into; the arrival of late-comers, etc.) but I am putting my attention where I want it to be. I could change this scene very easily by going on with the same dialogue about the Stanislavski system but, following with my eyes that man coming in late and sneaking up the balcony stairs, I could let him know what I think of tardiness. I could, in other words, divert my attention to wherever I wish in a scene, without changing the words at all. So you see it is a specific thing, to do with willful choice, that he is talking about in "Concentration."

Nineteen—"Feeling of truth (belief in what you do)." You might say that should also go without saying: of course you believe in what you do on the stage. But he doesn't mean being "sincere" in a general way. He means specifically the whole problem of generating the feeling of *faith* that comes from finding something true in what is happening that you can really believe in. This he felt was a basic element that good actors have and it ought to be possible to define that element so that one could work on it, and even find exercises to develop it. Since the situations and ideas of the authors that are given to us, as actors, to perform, can, from our own personal point of view, sometimes seem quite far-fetched, it is important that we find the way to believe in them. There is always *something* about them we can truly believe in, and to this we add our imagination.

Number Twenty is "The exchange of sentiments." There, he means the connection between two actors, or an actor and a group, or an actor and an object, while playing a scene. Even an actor who has no interest in anything like Stanislavski will say, "Look at me when I talk to you!" "Communion," it is called in *An Actor Prepares*, and it can be an inner feeling of connection even when we are not looking at our object.

Twenty-one: "To recreate emotion to show different colors." That is interesting for variety in playing. For example: I wanted to express my great enthusiasm for Jennie Tourel's song recital the other night to a musical friend. I had enjoyed it so much that I wailed, clapping my hand against my face, "I heard Jennie Tourel. How she sings! That woman! Such style! It was GREAT!!!" The way I wailed, anyone not understanding English might think I was describing an accident. I was "despairing" at how great an artist can be, instead of following the natural smiling exuberance that would ordinarily go with those words. I was using an emotional color entirely *opposite* to the natural one and, so, gained emphasis. One can do it the other way 'round too. You can say, quite happily, "I saw Joe on Television last night—was he terrible!"

The next item, Twenty-two, is a little subtle to go into here, but I think you actors will understand what is meant by "The fluid of the exchange of emotion." If you have ever been playing in a scene with an actor and the emotion has started to grow between the two of you and you have been able to sense it, measure it, and share it with the other artist, then you know what is meant by this item. The Lunts would probably, and justifiably, say, "Why, that's just playing together, dear!" Oh, well—let's press on.

Twenty-three. "The control that removes clichés (the judge of yourself)." Of course, sometimes one likes a nice cliché. What is meant, however, is that we should be on guard; at least we should know when we're using one and be able to decide not to, if we wish. The hand to the head for an "Oh, my Lord!" line, or the biting of the back of the hand for "terror," etc., are obvious physical clichés; our theatre is riddled with them. We have almost as many conventions as the Oriental theatre, in a way: the turning upstage with the hand covering the eyes when you cry. Or rather, when you *can't* cry. But, as in all of these items 11–27, (remember I'm still on the left, the "internal," side of the chart) Stanislavski means cliché *thinking* as well: the leaping to cliché conclusions as you work on your part.

Twenty-four: "The finishing of problems (beats) and mastery in movement" (again, he means *inner* movement). It is the knowledge that a certain section, a certain intention is over, that the next one is beginning, and just where that point comes in the part. It doesn't always come where the dialogue seems to indicate—especially in a well-written play. Just because the fellow says, "That's the last I'm going to say about that," doesn't mean he's through with that "beat." He may, in the next sentence, be talking about something seemingly different, but he still might be "trying to find out where you were with his wife last night." Even though he's changed the subject in the dialogue, you feel that the original intention is continuing to a certain further point that you and the director sense and have chosen. That control of the "inner movement" of your part is, I believe, what is referred to here.

"Theatrical personality and scenic sympathy (taking away the bad things that make bad personalities)." Number Twenty-five. There again, I don't think it refers too much to the problem of having a fine character (although a *little* of that wouldn't hurt!). I think it means the study of yourself, which so few people do, in order to know what you bring onto the stage as a personality. After all, that does become part, in some way, of the rôle you are creating. Very often actors fail to understand why they don't get a certain part, or why they are not successful in a part they do play. Quite frequently it has nothing to do with the acting, which may be perfectly adequate; but something is present in their own personalities that is either negating or distorting what is supposed to be there. So, says the Master, we should study our theatrical personalities, we should know what we, ourselves, bring onstage, what is useful in that, what could be corrected and what should be improved.

Twenty-six. "Ethical discipline (props, make-up, quarrels)." Well, we know that, to be a good artisan, one should take care of one's tools. As every violinist takes special care of his instrument, we, too, should feel something about our props and our make-up. Our dressing-room and back-stage behavior can easily affect our actual stage performance. Don't forget that I'm still on "the inside;" this item has to do with the proper atmosphere of creation.

The last item on the "internal" half of the chart, Number Twenty-seven, is "Tempo-rhythm." That's a tough one and I wish you would read about it in Stanislavski's books. "Tempo," of course, means fast or slow, and "rhythm" means the inner beat. This combination-term, Tempo-rhythm, refers to something Stanislavski worked on more and more toward the end of his life. It is tremendously interesting although difficult to describe quickly. In essence, he felt that while it is true that the proper psychological preparation for a part will make for proper rhythm, he also felt that finding the suitable tempo-rhythm of a character will *lead* you to feel correctly in the part, too. It is a double process. Any of you who were lucky enough to have seen Michael Chekhov in his uncle's one-act play about the impotent man living in an isolated cabin with his lusty wife will remember that his characterization was built on a kind of halting behavior and stuttering speech: an "impotent tempo-rhythm." Not only did this serve to give us a wonderful vocal as well as a physical image of impotence, but it also, I am sure, added to Mr. Chekhov's own *inner feeling* of impotence in his attempt to communicate with his wife, etc. We know, moreover, that we are often moved by experiences if we remember them in the rhythm in which they first happened. For an obvious example: you can have heard a song many times and then you suddenly hear it played in a certain tempo and it moves you. It may be that that is the way in which you first heard it under certain emotional circumstances and that same particular beat helps to move you again. Tempo-rhythm is, in this way, also related to "affective memory."

Now we come to Numbers Twenty-eight to Forty, which are the Processes of Expressing your Emotions. Did you notice the thrill in my voice when I read out those items before? I felt they needed a little emphasis these days.

Twenty-eight is "Relaxation." This is tremendously important to the actor because, when you have to play, everything conspires to tense your muscles, not the least being the fact that you're being looked at and judged: that "pull" of the audience. Stanislavski's point here is that it is more possible for whatever feeling you may have to come through and be delivered to the audience, if your body is in the correct state of physical relaxation. Tension has a tendency to press your feeling down and kill it, much like the bottle with the float in it with which, as children, we used to play. We'd press on the rubber end of the bottle and the little float would go down in the water and then come up again when we released the pressure. Therefore, if you have a tendency toward tension, as who doesn't at one time or another, there are exercises you can do (on the stage as well as in the classroom) to relax your muscles.

"External tempo and rhythm." Twenty-nine. This is related to number Twenty-seven. Just as our "feeling" affects the tempo and rhythm of our delivery, so our sense of external tempo and rhythm connects with our emotion. Acting training should include the development of our sense of time and sense of rhythm. It gets pretty tough in rehearsals when the point of the scene hangs on an actor's having a sense of rhythm and being able to come in on a certain swell in the action just right, on the beat, and say, "STOP!"—not to do it when he feels like stopping them, but to do it exactly on a certain syllable if he has to. You should, of course, know how to use tempo and rhythm creatively, within your part, and not just because you are told to go faster or slower. Certain characters, for example, speak faster than others and if you have to play one of those, you should be able to do it and not have to make him speak the way you do if you happen to be a slow speaker ordinarily, etc. Oh, are we going to come back to that one!

Thirty—"Placement of voice." You see Stanislavski cared about these things. Voice placement is extremely important. It is a great irritant, both to artist and public, if the voice is placed badly. But not only is all this important for good listening and intelligibility, but you should be able to place your voice where you want it for purposes of character. That may not be where it is ordinarily placed, and so you should study and know about your voice.

Number Thirty-one. "Diction (the feeling of the soul of the language by knowing the nature of sounds)." Isn't that nicely put? We should do a lot about this little number. Aside from the matter of pronunciation, there is the fact of what the use of the sound of words can give us. Some sounds are beautiful, some are ugly, still others are funny. If you have an appreciation of what the sounds of words convey, it can inspire your insides, too.

Number Thirty-two encompasses the "Rules of speaking: 1. Intonation 2. Pauses 3. Accent (to do design and get things from comma)." Yes, we're still on the Method! I am going to try to show what happens when all these aspects of acting are ridden over as unimportant in the cause of the actor himself "feeling fine" inside. I will also try to answer those who say that if you pay attention to these rules you cannot feel. Let's leave it at that for the moment.

Thirty-three. "The Sentiments of the Language." That means, I suppose, imagery: the actor's appreciation of the *ideas* of words and their combinations, their meanings and their evocations. We will return to this when we discuss the Method in relation to Poetic Theatre, Shakespeare, etc.

"Movement." Thirty-four. Well, that means your sense of where you are in the design of the scene, how you go from one place to another on the stage with a sense of design, as well as your actual knowledge of body expressiveness.

Number Thirty-five is "Dancing." Of course actual dancing can have practical use at times, say, if you are playing Molière and you are called upon to execute a real dance step. But even failing anything as specific as that (you don't have to become an accomplished ballet or tap dancer), I think any knowledge of dancing that you can have will help you in the creation of characters which require some sense of movement other than slouching around. We may even start to get some plays written in which we can use such interesting movement.

Thirty-six. "Fencing." What has that to do with acting? Well, when I was a kid in the Civic Repertory Theatre we studied it. Of course, we were playing *Romeo and Juliet* and we'd have been killed in the street brawls if we didn't know how to fence. Still it has a further value; the whole business of bodily coordination, the give and take, having to watch the other fellow's eye, the lightness and so on, are great aids for the actor.

"Sports" is Number Thirty-seven. A healthy body, in working order, ready for any physical command, Stanislavski felt, was an essential for the actor, too. So, sports.

Number Thirty-eight. "Acrobatics." This, he said, developed the actor's sense of "Decisiveness." The ability to leap into big moments fearlessly, without hesitation.

"Plastique" is the Thirty-ninth item. The ability to create an "unbroken line" of movement, triggered from within and culminating in outward plasticity. I'm sure Stanislavski must have noticed the beautiful Greek influence in

44

Duse's performances. She must have studied Greek sculpture. Yet it did not hinder her from being "real;" she had the reputation of being the "realest" actress of them all (her ability to blush, etc.). Still there isn't a photograph of her where the sculptured mold of the artist is not theatrical and beautiful.

Number Forty, the last item devoted to these means of expression is "The Way of Walking." Of course it could refer to various characteristic ways of walking, such as limping, or being bandylegged or pigeon-toed, etc. But I think he means something more than that. He felt that, for some reason or other, the tension of coming on the stage is such that people who were walking perfectly fine a second ago offstage, assume a stilted gait when they come on. (This "stagey" walk also could come from a wrong attitude toward acting in general.) To recapture simple, beautiful walking onstage, Stanislavski reexamined the whole process and set down a series of exercises. (Here, I feel he was inspired in a certain way by Isadora Duncan.) I remember once having hours of "walking" in a dance class with Tamiris during the Group Theatre days. We really consciously broke down the whole business of walking and finally got back to doing it again without thinking. By then, however, we had corrected many faults; we knew where our balance was, where the weight of our body pressed down, etc. It was quite fascinating. There's a section about walking in the book, *Building a Character*, in which Stanislavski really breaks the whole thing down into the various joints of the body, and so on. Well, it begins to get a little technical but, if you've seen some of the posturing and false ways of walking some actors fall into, you can see it is interesting to try to find some way to get back to walking simply and beautifully on the stage. Of course then, if you want to add some characteristic element of walking, you have your basis.

Two terms that are still undefined are "spine" and "long-distance mood," the last not appearing on the chart itself.

In *An Actor Prepares,* "spine" is referred to as the "Super-Objective." I think what Mr. Stanislavski meant by the "spine" of the play was something very much akin to what is called the "theme"—the underlying motivating idea that pervades the entire play. And each rôle in the play has *its* main objective deriving from the play's "Super-Objective." All the items on the chart serve this "spine."

For example: A play you all know, *Golden Boy,* by Odets, which the Group Theatre did, was about a violinist who, feeling inadequate in his surroundings for various reasons, and finding himself unable to cope with his problems, gave up his true calling as a musician in order to become a prize-fighter. Roughly, then, the director, Harold Clurman, said that the whole problem of the play, the "spine," was, "how to deal with the problems of life in a world where success is the criterion." Now everything in the play was about that in one way or another and each character in the play had a "spine" which was related to it. The young violinist felt that the way he could cope with this problem of feeling inferior was "to fight his way to the top," or as he says in the play, "to bang his way to the lightweight crown." The gangster in the play, on the other hand, felt that, by buying up everything and everybody, *he* could master this problem of being a success in a competitive world. This "hunting for possession" was his
46

single main objective all the way through his part. You can even have characters that may *seem* to be expressing quite the reverse of the "spine" of the play, but still are related. There was a comedy character in *Golden Boy*, a neighbor who felt that the only way he could cope was "to deride all success," and so all through the play he made fun of every aspect of success. When someone asked how he liked the big buildings of the city he answered, "And suppose they fall?" In one way or another, all through the play, in a comedic way, on an entirely different note from the "fight" of the leading character, he, too, was related to the main problem, the "Super-Objective" of the play. From the stated Spines one is able to choose proper intentions.

Now, "Long-distance Mood," for all its fancy sounding name, simply meant the all-pervading mood of a whole play, regardless of the various moods of the individual scenes. It is an important item. For example, in *Othello* there's a moment when *Othello* says to Iago, "O, blood, blood, blood!" and another in *Twelfth Night* when *Malvolio* says, "I'll be revenged on the whole pack of you." They are both in the mood of vengeance but it is not quite of the same calibre. In the first case, the all-pervading mood of the whole play is one of fateful tragedy, while the "Long-distance mood" of the second is that of a lark—even the title tells you that, *Twelfth Night,* or *What You Will.* There is a spirit of fun that affects *all* the many moods in the one, and a spirit of tragedy that affects all the moods in the other.

So much for definitions of terms.
Good night.

APRIL 29, 1957

SOME ATTITUDES TOWARD THE METHOD

I would like now to discuss various attitudes toward this monumental work of Stanislavski's. Recently, I have tried to think of my own attitude toward it. I find it is the same as what I feel toward *any* technique I have studied. There are two aspects to the way techniques are applied: the "unconscious guide" (mentioned before) as you create on the stage, and the conscious study in workshops or in learning a part.

This is as true for the director as for the actor. When a director prepares a production, analyzes the script, breaks the play down into its component parts, and decides on his production scheme, I think then, he too is consciously using the materials of the various techniques he has picked up. But quite a different process sets in when he is in the theatre in the heat of creation. I think back over my rehearsals and wonder if when I am sitting there, looking at the stage, listening, stopping the actors, correcting, do I ever actually use a technical formulation in my mind? I don't think so. The technical knowledge must be in me; but a kind of automatic process goes on as you create;

your "motor" is being fed by your technique. It is quite a different thing from *working on your technique*.

To test myself as to how technique has served me as I direct, I tried this week to think of specific moments when I had to have a certain effect; times when, as an artist, I was obsessed with a moment and it had to be done a specific way. I remembered, for example, a scene in *The Teahouse of the August Moon* when David Wayne and Johnny Forsythe were standing on a platform to address the natives of Okinawa who were gathered in the village square. I made a little design in my script where the people were to be placed. I got it all set on the stage with the characters closer or further away from David and Johnny, somebody turning away from them, but listening—you know, breaking it up a little! And after I had done everything seemingly needed for the scene and there it all was, I suddenly asked one character to lie on the ground, lean forward on one hand, turn up towards Johnny to listen, and curve his right leg all the way around back of him, making of his body a complete kind of circular line up toward the two central figures. The actor did it when he was placed there but every time we'd go through the scene, and he'd gotten up to say his few lines, he'd never return to his original position. He'd sit on his haunches to get comfortable; or if he did everything else right that leg never got all the way around back again. I kept saying, "Get the leg back!" I would not rest unless he did it just right. Believe me, I felt it was no good without that. (It reminds me of Boris Aronson, the designer, who once said at my house in the country when he saw a beautiful tree standing near a large rock, "Look at that tree—

52

without that rock it'd be nothing!" Of course, he was criticizing nature; this was only art that I was working on!) The actor finally said to me, "Why would I sit like that? It's uncomfortable for me and no one in the world would do it." So I said, "Look. He's a dancer—he's always posing." In my excitement I didn't even realize I was inventing; that the character wasn't a dancer at all, he was a painter! The point is that the actor was so happy to have *any* reason to do it that he believed me.

Now as I thought over that moment this past week I tried to find out where that idea of staging came from. Various memories started coming back to me. I remembered a lecture I'd heard about Meyerhold and his theory of "centering;" one actor centers others by the way in which he places himself before them. I said, "I wonder if that's what I was trying to do?" Then I thought, "It's also something I've seen in painting; you look at a scene and there is some force that leads you to where your eye is supposed to go. Do I know it from painting?" The point is that sometime that technical knowledge entered my consciousness and in a moment of work it emerged to be used. That is my attitude toward the use of all techniques, including this Stanislavski system. It is all there to know about and to study and to use when, and if, the need arises. But I would now like to go on to some other attitudes toward this Method.

First, let's take Stanislavski's own attitude towards his Method, to which he devoted his long life. By the way, in a letter I received this week an actor said, "Well, from just what you've said so far of the Method, it would take a whole lifetime to perfect oneself in it!" All I can say in

53

answer to that is, yes, of course it would. If you are an artist, it invariably takes you a whole lifetime to perfect whatever it is you're trying to do, and you always die too young. Stanislavski was always searching, always changing, and he said, "It is not *my* system. I did not invent anything. I am simply trying to put down something which is based on the laws of creation." He religiously studied those laws in his own work and in the performances of great actors. Still, he was very reluctant to publish his books on his Method. Mrs. Hapgood, the translator, had a time getting him to agree to have the books printed at all because Stanislavski felt that was too *final*. And to his Group Theatre visitors in 1934, he said, "If the System doesn't help you, forget it." Then he added, "But perhaps you do not use it properly." Even at the end, when he was dying, he was experimenting in his idea of tempo-rhythm with a wheel of different-colored electric light bulbs. He watched this wheel as it turned in different tempi to see what effect color and movement would have on emotion. So it certainly ill-behooves us to be too dogmatic about our interpretations of his Method.

Take Michael Chekhov, for instance, who visited the Group actors during the thirties when his company was here. We had a party for him and he came and spoke with us. We had heard of Stanislavski's remark to Gordon Craig, "If you want to see my System working at its best go to see Michael Chekhov tonight. He's playing some one-act plays by his uncle." We were waiting for this actor, as you can imagine. And here he was in the same room with us; we could talk to him. But whenever we asked him a question about Stanislavski, he'd say, "I can't answer that fairly. I haven't been in contact with him for several years —and he was always changing." The acknowledged favorite of the Master would not commit himself at all!

Parenthetically, Chekhov himself observed all of the "externals" as well as the "internals" in his acting. He did not emphasize one to the exclusion of the other; his acting was absolutely complete, inside and out. If any of you were lucky enough to see him in *The Inspector General,* you will remember he had a physical characterization that was the envy of any dancer. Although he was a short man, in this part he had a line to his body which made him seem very tall; he walked on his toes, his hands were extended, and to make them longer, gloves dangled from them. He was playing a fop and he had the look, movement and sound of a fop down brilliantly. Yet, when he had to be drunk in the party scene, he didn't do a lot of drunken movements; he got so drunk *inside* that it was positively catching. I remember very well that, when the curtain came down on that scene, we all arose from our seats and staggered up the aisle, quite intoxicated!

Chekhov himself, going on from Stanislavski, worked on what he called "psychological gesture." To give you an example, *The Deluge,* in which he played, was a kind of morality play, and had a lot of mean people, all hating each other, gathered in a bar. At the end of the first act somebody announced, "The dam has broken! We're all going to be drowned!" So when the curtain went up on the second act, since these people believed they were only going to live a short while, all their "fine feelings" for each other came out. One told the other how much he'd always liked him and how sorry he was for whatever he'd done wrong. Chekhov was playing an American business man. He had bickered and fought with his partner all through the first act but now, in the second act, he was going to try to make it up. So he sat down with his partner and tried to tell him that it wasn't that he'd hated him, that it was the fault of the business, and that he'd really always loved him. His partner wouldn't believe him so he kept trying to prove he'd loved him. As Chekhov was talking, his hands started to dig into the man's heart. Suddenly one got this terrific image of what love is—the wanting to become *one* with somebody. It was a great moment of imaginative acting. He was feeling it all inside to the full, but he had chosen a way to express it which was brilliant.

In a lecture in New York, Chekhov gave some other examples of "psychological gesture" from his past performances. In *Erik XIV* he played the weak king and he demonstrated how he had to give a loud order, calling for his soldiers. As he did it, he made a powerful gesture which ended, however, very weakly, and he frightened himself with his own voice. From that moment alone, you knew everything about that character. That single combination of gesture, sound and feeling did it. In his stage acting Michael Chekhov embodied the "Complete Internal" plus the "Complete External" outlined in the Method chart, yet he was reticent to call himself a Stanislavski authority. We should emulate this attitude by trying always to examine the subject undogmatically.

Now there was a distinct change in attitude toward the Method in 1934 when my Group Theatre friends came back with the report from Stanislavski. That change had to do with the over-emphasis on certain aspects of the Method, a situation that has cropped up again with latter-day exponents. One item in particular which had been very much emphasized in the early thirties was the "affective memory." It was subsequently found that one's insides could often be attuned by more simple and more immediate means. For example, the ideas in the play itself; one can get a good deal from really listening to the play. Don't forget that in the first reading of a play you are often very moved, and very correctly, at that. If you seek what it was that affected you that first time, you might arrive more safely at feelings that fit the play. It was also found that the complete performance of the "intentions" (which is something one can accomplish with one's mind and will) with all of the circumstances of the play and the particular scene present, leads to correct emotion. Also the *choice* of stimulating intentions was important. Then, there's the "as if" that I spoke of last week; to ask yourself, "What is the *nature* of this moment? What do *I* understand by it?" That proved tremendously stimulating because it opened up the imagination and the imagination is a great emotional stimulant for the actor. All these things, more readily accessible and easier to control, can produce natural emotional responses. I suppose in very high moments and where proper preparation is difficult, one could still fall back on "affective memory." I myself, in my work with actors over the years, have found that emotion is not necessarily the biggest problem. If I have chosen my actors carefully and everything else has been prepared, I usually find the actors are "feeling" correctly. And how some actors love to cry, too! I find myself constantly saying, "Try not to cry as long as possible." I keep pulling

57

them back—but there's still a lot of crying! And there's still a lot of "working for emotion." That is why one occasionally notices in performances some emotional agitation going on in the actor; but what it is about is not always clear. It often seems to be mere self-indulgence, more like *emotionalism* than emotion, a kind of self-induced feeling which is more closely related to pathology than to art. Crying, after all, is not the sole object of acting. If it were, my old Aunt Minnie would be Duse!

Besides, this Method, or any theatre technique that you study, is not only for serious playing. There is everything in the theatre: light comedy, farce, etc. Well, what about farce? The other day an actor said to me, "I am in a farce and one evening in a performance I did something different with my hand. Suddenly I looked at it and thought, 'Oh, oh, that's wrong at this moment. I shouldn't do it,' and it stopped me cold. It killed my sense of fun." And he blamed his studying for this. "Well," I said, "Not only are you not supposed to stop and think of your technique in a farce, you are not supposed to do it in a tragedy either! You work out your part and then you play it! It is two different things! When you are in Carnegie Hall playing your Beethoven Piano Sonata, you can't stop and think in the middle of a run, 'I'd better put my thumb under my third finger or else I'll never make it!' If you did that you couldn't play! The work that you have done in preparation, the technique you have invested in your creation, should not be a preventive. If it is, it is worthless." In Ruth Gordon's magnificent farcical performance in *The Matchmaker*, I saw nothing inconsistent with the truthful approach that Stanislavski indicated. Her playing even seemed improvisational; and in a farce where everything is always worked out to the split-second. It was very funny, but also very true, and even touching at times.

To continue the search for an explanation of other prevalent attitudes toward the Method I'd like to check dates again. The first book, *An Actor Prepares*, which was concerned with the "internal," was published in 1936. The second, *Building a Character*, dealing mainly with the "external," or the method of expressing one's feelings, was published in 1949. Now, although they were conceived together and meant to be thought of together, there is a separation of thirteen years in the publishing dates. I wonder how many hangovers there are now of what was thought about, taught and studied during those thirteen years. I must say that in the Group Theatre, where this technique was studied in the '30's, there were always experiments in style going on along with the "psychological" work. I know I had a class in 1933 in the basement of the Broadhurst Theatre, where we were doing *Men in White*, in which I was attempting to find some approach to style in acting through experiments with music, painting, etc. John Garfield was in that class and I remember he worked out a number based on a painting by Picasso of a shepherd boy. He just started from that with no psychological idea— just the painting. He studied it and tried to recreate, with his body, the exact figure of the shepherd boy—the stance, the look, everything. Then he started to make it move; he imagined how that boy would walk, sit, gesture, and slowly he started to build a character based on that painting. He then chose the kind of a voice that would fit the boy, and gradually added some words, a suitable poem, I believe. He eventually worked up a beautiful, lyrical scene.

My mind leaps from that étude to the results which so many now think derive from any contact with the Method: the old "mumbling, but with feeling" business. Let me just read you something here from *Building a Character* on mumbling:

"The nature of certain sounds, syllables and words requires a clipped pronunciation comparable to eighth and sixteenth notes in music: others must be produced in a more weighty, longer form, more ponderously, like whole or half notes. Along with this some sounds and syllables receive a stronger or a weaker rhythmic accentuation; a third group may be entirely without any accent.

"These spoken sounds, in turn, are interlarded with pauses, rests for breathing, of most variable lengths. All these are phonetic possibilities out of which to fashion an endless variety of the tempo-rhythms of speech. In making use of them an actor works out for himself a finely proportioned speech style. He needs this when he is on the stage and using words to convey both the exalted emotions of tragedy and the gay mood of comedy . . . A measured resonant, well-blended speech possesses many qualities akin to those of music and singing.

"Letters, syllables, words—these are the musical notes of speech, out of which to fashion measures, arias, whole symphonies. There is good reason to describe beautiful speech as musical." By the way, you know who the author is—Stanislavski! To continue:

"Words spoken with resonance and sweep are more affecting. In speech as in music there is a great difference between a phrase enunciated in whole, quarter or sixteenth notes, or with triplets or quintuplets thrown in. In one case the phrase can be solemn, in another the tripping chatter of a school girl.

"In the first instance there is calm, in the second nervousness, agitation.

"Talented singers know all about this. They stand in fear of sinning against rhythm. If the music calls for three quarter-notes a true artist will produce three tones of exactly that length. If the composer has put a whole note, the true singer will hold it to the end of the bar. If the music calls for triplets or syncopations, he will sing them with the mathematical rhythm required. This precision has an irresistible effect. Art requires order, discipline, precision and finish. Even in cases where one is called upon to convey a rhythmic effect musically, one must do it with clear-cut finish. Even chaos and disorder have their tempo-rhythm.

"What I have just said in regard to music and singers is equally applicable to us dramatic artists. There exists, however, a vast number of singers who are not real artists but just people who sing, with or without voices. They have an astonishing facility for jumbling eighth with sixteenth-notes, quarter with half-notes, three eighth-notes of equal length into one, and so on.

"Consequently their singing lacks all necessary precision, discipline, organization, finish. It turns into a disorderly, chaotic mess. It ceases to be music and becomes some sort of sheer vocal exhibitionism.

"The same thing can and does happen to speech. Take

61

an actor, for instance, of the type of (here he mentions the fellow's name) with an uneven rhythm in his speech. He switches it not only from clause to clause but in the middle even of a single phrase. Often one half of a sentence will be spoken in a slow tempo and the second half in a markedly rapid one. Let us take the phrase, 'Most potent, grave and reverend signiors.' That would be spoken slowly, solemnly, but the next words, 'my very noble and approved good masters,' would be, after a long pause, suddenly delivered with extreme rapidity.

"Many actors who are careless of speech, inattentive to words, pronounce them in such thoughtless, slipshod speed, without putting any endings on them, that they end up with completely mutilated, half-spoken phrases." So much for blaming mumbling on Stanislavski.

In justice, I want to read the end of that chapter, in which he also says, "A clear-cut rhythm of speech facilitates rhythmic sensibility and the opposite is also true: the rhythm of sensations experienced helps to produce clear speech. Of course, all this occurs in the cases where precision of speech is thoroughly based on inner suggested circumstances and the 'magic if.'" Now it is the present emphasis on this latter section to the detriment of the former that I am talking about on this platform.

When Stanislavski, as an old man, came to Paris he was invited to a small theatre to watch a rehearsal. As he didn't know where the stage door was he came through the front of the house. Since the company was rehearsing on the stage and he didn't want to interrupt he sat in the back of the auditorium for a moment. The director was sitting down front in the house and the actors were on the stage rehearsing but Stanislavski couldn't hear anything. So he got up from the seat and moved halfway down in the house and he still couldn't hear anything. Finally annoyed, he got right down in the front with the director who recognized him and said, "Oh, Maestro, you're here!"

"Yes, I'm here," said Stanislavski. "By the way, what is that you're doing up there?"

"Why, Maestro," replied the director, "we are practicing your Method!"

I think the theory of such zealous partisans must be that in attempting to agitate the emotional juices of the actor, a sort of psychological constipation sets in, preventing the free flow of speech. But speech can be beautified, not destroyed, by true feeling! What's more, there are many non-Method actors who mumble; and I can also give you examples of actors who do nothing inconsistent with Stanislavski's aims and who, no matter what else you may think, I know you would agree have good loud voices.

The same canard is spread around about singing. That is: you can't sing if you have real feeling; it chokes up your voice, your production. Yet the greatest operatic singers in history were all "true feelers." The famous singer Chaliapin was a mountain of feeling. In our own time Boris Christoff, whom I've heard in Italy, sings with wonderful, well-understood feeling, and sings beautifully, what's more. In my own work in *Regina*, which was a grand opera, at the City Center, I had Brenda Lewis in the leading part and in working with her I found feeling never impeded her singing. On the contrary, her emotion colored and enhanced her singing. The whole point is: what kind of a sound do you want to make: do you want to make a pretty, even, empty sound; or do you want to make a sound of *true* beauty because it has to do' with what's going on in the play?

See you next week.

MAY 6, 1957

METHOD FETISHES

For the past three weeks we have talked a good deal about "Method." Now tonight—let's talk a little about "Madness"! For example, as we ended last week we were talking about people who think a beautiful voice or good diction cannot be achieved if disturbed by real feeling and, conversely, those who think real feeling cannot arise if it is disturbed by considerations of voice, diction, or other problems of physical characterization.

It seems to me that the unreasoning addiction to both of these attitudes produces a number of fetishes. We have already indicated the fetish some people make of emotion. Of course some of these self-styled Stanislavski exponents of "real feeling," those who tilt the scale too much toward the emphasis of digging for emotion, defend themselves by dabbling in problems of speech, movement and so on. However, they never really work at it with the dogged devotion they give to problems of psychology. And any singer or dancer will tell you that dogged devotion is what is needed to develop one's voice or body. For example, in criticizing a scene done in a workshop, the instructor will criticize and discuss the content of the scene, the relationships of the people to each other, the understanding of the points in the scene, whether the actor has achieved the feeling of the character, and whether the feeling the actor had was real or simulated. How many times will the instructor say, "Your voice doesn't carry! Stage-energy is higher than life-energy."? Now it may be that with work done in small rooms the problem of voice projection is not apt to arise, but it is a major problem when you try out that tender play in the Shubert Theatre in Philadelphia! There are dangers likewise in holding rehearsals in cozy little rehearsal halls where the chairs are closely placed and the actors are seated together happily "connecting" with one another and "feeling truth" as the boy softly breathes to the girl, "Why didn't you tell me you felt that way about me?" Then, after a few happy weeks, you arrive in New Haven and get on the stage. The boy stands away up left, on a mountain, and the girl is away down right, in the valley. Behind them is the designer's marvellous sky with clouds moving across it and the lighting man has thrown beautiful shadows on the faces of the actors. Everything is going fine and then the boy turns toward the girl and says, "   ?" The director comes running down the aisle shouting, "Beautiful! Just beautiful —but you forgot to say your lines." The actor may say, and quite correctly too, "Look, I did it that way for weeks during rehearsals. It's in me solid and I feel it that way. If I start to 'talk up' now I will shatter the sense of truth that I've built up." Well, we will try to show how *teaching* and *rehearsing,* to be valid, must take in the actual problems of *performing* in public.

Then again, how often, in criticism, does an instructor

say, "You are speaking too fast. You did not pronounce the 'd' at the end of the word. By not pronouncing the 'd' you have changed the tense. In changing the tense you have changed the plot because it sounds as if you're saying, 'I kill him!' when you are supposed to be saying, 'I killed him!' If you say it the first way we think you may or may not do it; but if you say it the second way we know you did it, and that is the story of the play." It may be just a little "d," but often a scene has been misinterpreted by just such little things as that. It may seem funny to you but I am sure there are authors sitting here tonight who aren't laughing!

Another fetish that has been made from the Method in some quarters is the one about terminology. It has created a kind of dogma out of what should have been a freeing principle. For example, there is a whole taboo that exists about giving line readings. Says the actor to the director, "Don't give me the line reading! Just tell me what it is you want and let me do it in my own way!" And yet so many times the simple point is that the line *has* to be said in a certain way in order to make the point; if it is said any other way, with all the good will (and all the feeling) in the world, the point is just simply not made. Again let Stanislavski defend himself:

"Let us take an example from Pushkin. It is possible to say—
I have a gilded *monument* to myself erected;
I have a gilded monument to myself erected;
I have a gilded monument to *myself* erected;
I have a gilded monument to myself *erected;*
or finally,
I have a *gilded* monument to myself erected.

"And in each case the meaning will be different, in accordance with the word we desire to emphasize. The emphatic word is the centre of attraction. In it the whole meaning of the sentence is hidden, and as a result of the combination of attention, strength of the voice, and the amount of feeling put into it, the feeling-thought-word the actor expresses is capable, like a spark, of kindling the enthusiasm of a crowd." The point is that he does not say "feeling" alone, he makes a triple word out of it—"feeling-thought-word."

Another fetish of terminology is that we should never use nouns to describe "intentions." You shouldn't act a noun ("suspicion") because it is a state of being, a result; what you should do is to have some desire or wish ("to find out if he did it") and the product of that intention would be a state of suspicion. Well, and good, but you can imagine my relief at finding out that if I couldn't think of a verb fast enough while working and could only think of a noun, there was no policeman around to arrest me! How happy I was when I got out into the big world and worked with artists in other fields, who had lots of involved terminology in their work too, and found it quite possible to say, as I once did, for example, to Virgil Thomson, "Look, I need four bars of fast music here." And he replied, "Loud or soft?" We both knew what we were talking about; I didn't have to say, "Agitato con passione!" I was also greatly relieved at reading Stanislavski's own directing script of *Othello* when it was published in 1949. After *Iago* tells *Othello* he would like to be *Cassio's* undertaker, *Othello* says, "Excellent good." But in his director's book, next to that line, did the Master write, "to exult in the thought of vengeance?" No! Written down there, in Stanislavski's hand, it says, "Great animation bordering on joy." Now how unStanislavski can you get! Also, it is full of remarks such as, "pause of anxiety." What would lead a purist quicker to "indicating a result" than a "pause of anxiety?" Of course Stanislavski knew what he meant and, I am sure, was able to get his actors to do that truthfully. But I was glad to see that the Master could use improper terminology too—or was it simply that he was not making a fetish of his own system! I had always said, "Call it spinach if you must, call it anything as long as you *do* it." I was glad for the corroboration.

In *My Life in Art*, Stanislavski said on this point, "The actors carefully questioned me about the special terminology which was used by us during the study of the system. This was accompanied by one error on my part and on the part of the actors for which I am still paying, and heavily. To say the truth, not only the actors, but even the pupils of the Studio had accepted the system more or less on trust. They learned the terms, and then they used the terminology to cover their own perceptions which were at times creative, but mostly merely theatrical. The majority of them were the old well-known artificial habits, filled with theatricality and theatrical stencils. They were accepted to be that New of which the system talked. But the continuous exercises, like those of the singer who works day in, day out, over the placing and development of sound, like those of the violinist or 'cellist who develops in himself a true artistic tone, like those of the pianist who works over the technique of the fingers and the position of the hand, like those of every dancer who prepares his body for plastics

71

and dancing, were conspicuous by their absence, and have never been performed even up to the present day, either by the actors or the pupils of the Studio. This is why I claim that my system has not yet shown any of its real results. Many learned to concentrate, but this only made them make all their old mistakes and made those mistakes display themselves more and more, perfected those mistakes, so to say. But the actor feels himself in comfort on the stage in that way, and he accepts this customary incorrectness of theatrical mood for the natural living over of his part. Such actors are convinced that they are living over their parts, that they have understood all, that my system has brought them unusual help, and they touchingly thank me and praise me for the discovery of a new America. But—'I will find but ill health in that praise.' " That was written in 1924—quite prophetic.

Conversely, some who would maintain they understood the Method not at all, might actually perform in a way that does the Master proud. Every time one has a discussion on this subject, the name of Laurette Taylor comes up; she is admired and pointed to by adherents of the Stanislavski system. I was fortunate enough to have spent some time with her—naturally I went to see her and study her often on the stage and I heard her lecture, too—but I also went to her apartment and sat with her to pick her brains. She was very generous in that way to anyone who was interested. I asked her a lot of questions as to what she did when working out a part. I sat stunned a good deal of the time as I listened to her describing in minute detail the exact physical patterns she planned for herself in a part. I remembered how she actually appeared to be when she came out on the stage, seemingly meeting those people for the first time, not knowing how either they or she got there, with that wonderful kind of "lost" quality which gradually grew in understanding throughout the play. What she *said* was really almost the opposite of what she *did;* what she did was what she, as a great actress, knew subconsciously. And, in art, what you say you do is often quite different from what you do.

Laurette once gave a talk to some actors in which she described what she thought were the ingredients of great acting. I remember that she stood perfectly still on the stage the entire time; she didn't gesture at all as she spoke about the various things she felt were important: imagination, etc. At the very end, her closing remark was, "But above all, the most important thing to remember," and here she assumed a remarkably grandiose pose, one hand flung high in the air, "is to be simple!" It was an absolute miraculous moment, unforgettable, with that sense of balance all great artists have. It was the one place she felt she couldn't afford to be simple, that she had to do something to drive that point about simplicity home!

The same principle holds for directors, too. The difference between the first production-plan talk and what happens when the curtain goes up on opening night may be the widest chasm in all geography. The director might say, in his production talk, "We're going to make this entire production have the quality of a fog!" It could be a perfectly reasonable production idea, but unless there is a specific plan to do the play behind a scrim, to blow on dry ice across the stage, to have the actors walking around as though they were in a fog, for the actors to "think foggily," or *something*, it remains so much talk.

Those artists, then, who make a fetish of the Method, should know that what is good in *any* idea must enter into us and then express itself naturally in work. We must search for new aspects of the idea too, and in doing so, we pay real homage to the innovator who was always probably doing the same thing. We must also study all new techniques, thus constantly expanding our understanding of fundamental beliefs. In *My Life in Art*, speaking of his system, Stanislavski said, "It does good only when it becomes the second nature of the actor, when he stops thinking of it consciously, when it begins to appear naturally, as of itself." This answers the question so many actors ask, "What about spontaneity? How can you be spontaneous if you have to think of technical things?" I quote, in further evidence, from *Conversations with Casals* (the great Catalan musician)—Question: "Do you think discipline and spontaneity can work together?" Answer: "In every branch of art, as well as in music, the work of preparation ruled by discipline should finally disappear, so that the elegance and freshness for the form should strike us as being spontaneous."

Why are so many actors who have studied in the Method recognizable for their technique rather than for the part they are supposedly playing? Well, for one thing, you can always see them "concentrating" very hard—regardless of the particular amount of concentration needed. This gives, in my view, a false sense of importance to the wrong things, with a resultant heaviness. It is true of directors

74

too. Occasionally, in a scene, one doesn't know *where* to look, it's all so important. There is no focus, no design, no art! Even a photographer "arranges" life before he snaps his shutter.

Then, too, you see these devoted actors pursuing an objective through to its finish unheedful of the obvious life around them (very un-Stanislavskiish, by the way). This gives the appearance of a kind of inexplicable blindness. In short, their technique is showing. Good artists don't do this. When we are part of an audience watching a performer we don't want to think, "This performance must have cost about $750.00 in lessons at Mme. So-and-so's." We want to feel as we did the other night at Jennie Tourel's concert when she sang the Schumann song cycle. We felt: that is probably just the way Schumann would have wanted it sung; that he'd have been very happy to have heard it like that, such was her devotion to every aspect of the words and the music. We were not unmindful of her phenomenal technique, but we blessed her for using it as a means and not as an end.

Another reason that some actors, in performance, seem "Methody," or inexplicably involved, is that their approach is *too* analytical. I hit that "too" because I don't want to give the impression that I feel one should not analyze one's part or the play. However, I feel that often not enough trust is put in the play. If it is a good play, its clues will jump out at you and stimulate you. A good play will also play a great deal of itself *by* itself if you will let it. As a director I understand the problem because when I started directing I used to work out absolutely everything before I came to my first rehearsal; I didn't trust the actors, the play, or myself most of all. My first worry was that I would not have enough time. How could I possibly do all that was required in four weeks? I had heard stories of the Habima Theatre's production of *The Dybbuk*, which they had rehearsed for six months, and the last three months they had to rush! The author of the play was ill (not because it was taking them six months—he was ill anyway) and they wanted to get the play on while he was still alive. Unfortunately, on the night of the dress rehearsal, he died.

There were other anecdotes too. When Stanislavski came to this country with the Moscow Art Players, he went to see some shows on Broadway. One of the shows he saw was *The Goat Song*, which he enjoyed. After the play he went backstage and said to the actors, "The performance was just marvellous! How long did you rehearse it?" "Four weeks." "It was no good!"

So, I was thoroughly prepared in advance and worked very fast in the rehearsals of my first Broadway production, *My Heart's in the Highlands*, and at the end of the first week I was ready to open. Everything was finished! I was afraid to tell anybody I had nothing more to do. I was also afraid to keep repeating it and repeating it for three more weeks because the performance would be stale. I didn't know what to do. Well, fortunately there were a lot of children in the play and we played games. It was Easter time too so, one day, we had a very nice Easter egg hunt. It was on the stage of the old Guild Theatre (now the ANTA) on 52nd Street; I don't think they ever had an Easter egg hunt there before, or since.

Now, putting the wrong emphasis on certain aspects, at the expense of others, in teaching the Method, leads to the trouble that turns up later in production. I know some actors who have studied for years and yet when they come to work in an actual production, they have no useful technique. One: they have no sense of rhythm. (If you want to be corny, you can say "timing," but since I'm a lecturer now, I'll say rhythm.) Once, in a play, I had to have a fellow say to a crowd, "Come on!" and they had to reply three times, "No!" It had to go like this: "Come on!" "No!" "COME ON!!" "NO!!" *"COME ON!!!"* *"NO!!!"* For that scene, I *had to* have him build it dynamically. He had to do the second, "Come on!" louder and faster than the first, and the third louder and faster than the second or I had no build, no excitement, no scene. Well, he just could not do it. He was very *real,* and very busy, but he was saying, "Aww come onnnnnn!" to the crowd, and so they found themselves answering, "Aww noooooo!" The whole thing was just awful.

Two: they have no sense of movement. I had a scene where a fellow had to catch up a girl as she ran toward him and carry her off high over his head. He dropped her —every time! Finally I said, "I will fix this so you can't miss her. Now look, she will run toward you and on such and such a word she will jump. You don't have to worry about anything; you don't have to think of a thing except that word. The second she says that word you be ready to catch her and then it will work." He dropped her again! Finally, her husband objected, "You are killing my wife. This is past the realm of art!" From the standpoint of mercy, this actor just had to be fired!

Three: no ability to do small problems easily and unobtrusively. Let's think about this for a moment because it is fundamental and very important. I suspect there is a danger inherent in the practice of working exclusively on "big" scenes in studio classes. It is inevitable that you will choose an exciting scene to do and not a dreary scene where nothing much happens. You're not going to take the trouble to meet with someone and rehearse for hours on a scene where you come in and say, "Give me a cigarette, Joe" and your partner answers, "Just a minute, I'll go and get one." What you will probably do is pick a good scene out of a play where someone cries, or strangles somebody, or does something dramatic. This continuous immersion in the most emotional, violent, and exciting scenes makes picking up a glass and going to the sink to get a drink a big bore and, somehow, not *acting*. Yet a part is really composed of a whole series of that kind of thing. How many "big" scenes are there in a play? And how much of one's part is often sloughed off because of the inability to execute those "small" aspects of it? If possible, it is naturally preferable to work on a whole part when studying in a workshop; even if you don't execute the whole part you should really work it out. Now, in defense, you might say, "What about singers? Singers take arias out of operas and study them, don't they?" My answer is, yes they do. But I can only point out that I think the same danger exists for them. When they come to the performance of the complete opera the arias are usually quite unrelated to the whole and are done as showpieces. You should want your acting to be related to the *whole* play, to the author, to the style of the play, and to all the other actors present, and not only to that one scene and that one person that you have as your partner in the scene class. A dancer is not someone who can only execute fast turns brilliantly but someone who can walk, or move slowly, or stand still!

Four: the ability to "justify" what is required in the scene regardless of your personal desire to do it some other way. This is a big subject. It's the "I-don't-feel-it-that-way" problem! Sometimes the exigencies of the moment demand that a line be said in a certain way: let's say loudly. The reasons for this can be manifold—a matter of balance, of emphasis, of shock. It may be a need of the director, of the other actor in the scene, of the construction of the scenery, or what not. But our purist actor says that anything over a whisper here will violate his true feeling! What about all the other truths present? A truthful moment on the stage is made of many components. It should be possible for the actor to use his technique to do what is required of him and not allow his technique to prevent him from doing it. One can always find a *justification* that will permit one to do what is wanted by the production and still satisfy the inner man.

The next subject of the Method often misinterpreted is *improvisation*. Improvisation, defined simply, means playing a scene in your own words instead of those of the author. There is, in my view, the danger that, instead of achieving a sense of "freedom," improvisation can lead to a looseness of form. It can lead to playing "yourself" at the expense of the character rather than searching for the character in yourself. Actually, improvisation is the *control of the problem*. I use the word "problem" here to mean the intention of the scene. As you improvise, you must observe the inner *form* of the scene, where one section ends and another begins.

Improvisation does have certain specific values but I believe it should be used sparingly and only for certain definite results. I have used it, for example, to force a connection, a relationship, between two people working in a play when I couldn't get them to do it, for one reason or another, any other way while saying their lines in the play. Whatever the reason was, I could not get them to talk or listen to each other and really play the scene in the author's words. So I said, "Now that you know the make-up of the scene, the intentions, just get up and do it in your own words. Forget the lines of the play; if some lines do happen to come to you, say them, don't try *not* to say them." As soon as they finished, I made them go right back and do the same scene *with* the author's lines, trying to retain what they gained from that little improvisation. But you must watch and insist that the problems of the scene are executed, the inner form retained, and that they don't ramble and say, "Did I tell you of the time my grandfather—." That's the prevalent danger. (This is an example of what I said earlier on the uses of a technique. If you need something and haven't been able to get it, you reach for a technical element, use it, and then get right on with the show again.)

There are other uses of improvisation, too, which can give fine results that cannot be obtained any other way. For instance, there may be certain necessary physical elements of characterization you simply can't get from the play itself. Suppose you had to play a coal-miner but there is no scene in the coal mine. The play takes place in the kitchen or living room. Now you are far from being a coal-miner and you don't know what being in the mines all day does to you physically; or mentally, for that matter. Well, you can, as an étude, do an exercise perhaps that doesn't have any words in it, but in which you go through the activities of someone who has to crawl through a very low place, where it is very dark, and so on. When you have finished that you might have some sense of where your bones hurt when you come home at night to that kitchen, how your eyes have to slowly get adjusted to light, etc. In that way, you get real value from an improvisation because you are working for a solution to a particular problem.

Workshop training should also always be related to playing, and not carried on in an academic vacuum. Some of the views finicky people have regarding speech training for example, that it might lead to "precious" speech may very well be justified if the training is isolated; but that does not mean one shouldn't have speech training at all. It is quite possible to have lessons in speech that are really integrated with the acting problem. Failing that, it is possible to have simple speech training from a person who knows nothing about the acting process at all and, if you are watched over by somebody in your workshop, or by yourself, if you do know about it, to use that training in your acting without "destroying" your insides. Suppose, in rehearsing a part, you have the problem of an accent. If you have no natural flair for it, you have to really break it down, study it, the rhythm, etc. First, you read the scene without accent so you get an understanding of it. You then start working, just mechanically, on the accent and try to break it down. You have to do that just as you have to find out where your balance is before you can dance; technical and mechanical though it is, you just have to do it! As soon as you've done a little work like that, go immediately back again to playing the scene and let whatever is left of your accent work itself in. At this point you're not thinking of the accent, but just doing your scene. Enough of the accent will rub off. Perhaps you will lose some of it, but there will be enough. As you continue to work you can keep your eye, or rather, ear on it. It is just like the limbering-up exercises dancers do; inherent in those exercises are the movements they use in their dancing, but the exercises do not *prevent* them from dancing well. So, too, there is no reason why that same kind of work should prevent you from acting well.

A lot of talk is heard about "animal exercises" that go on in acting workshops—somebody is "making like a monkey." Well, the fact of the matter is that when you discuss any part (or person) you very often talk in some terms of imagery. Even in a realistic play you say that this character is slippery as an eel, or that that girl has the air of a gazelle, or that this fellow walks like a bear. These are general elements of characterization. It's quite possible for you to work out some characterization of a guy who is heavy, gross, and tired, and who walks like a bear, with his arms hanging. You have observed a bear, and you think that is a good image for this part. It is an element of characterization which you can incorporate in your character. You can go further; you can become even more specific in your usage of this kind of character element. Do you remember Charles Laughton in the end of *Henry VIII* when he becomes senile? There was a scene where he

Mr. Lewis directing a scene from *Brigadoon,* with Agnes de Mille, the show's choreographer.

was eating his supper; if you will check the picture you will notice that he must have been working from some image of a squirrel because he ate with quick tiny little bites, and his eyes were darting back and forth like a little ferreted animal.

Now, if you have any element of characterization such as a lisp, a stammer, a limp, or a squint, you may want to practice it, because you should be able to do it easily, so that it becomes part of your acting. You can work on exercises in animal characterizations just as you would for any other physical aspect of a part in order to pick out some element that you will incorporate into your characterization.

I have seen people do this kind of exercise for the purpose of simply stimulating the imagination of the actor generally and I think *that* is where all the funny stories come from. I agree that you can go too far in that sort of thing if you never apply the results practically. But if you have a specific objective in mind, or something that you are actually going to use in a part and you know how to incorporate it into acting, I think it is something that is as valuable as any other kind of characterization work.

Now, to finish up this particular list of misconceptions of the Method and bring it 'round full circle again to the problem of mumbling. There is an actor that I know who has very real feeling and is a sensitive and truthful actor *until* he speaks—then he empties out. I have watched him play, and when he is in a scene listening to somebody or thinking of something he is marvellous. Then he speaks and it is like pressing a button that just empties this feeling out.. His "beautiful" command of speech is "disconnected." That is the opposite side of the coin of those who can't speak well because they are so moved!

What is the answer? What really is a beautiful voice? Is it a pretty sound with good diction and emptiness inside? No. I think Laurette Taylor had a beautiful voice (I have a phonograph record of her, too, to prove it). It was a very lovely and easy voice production that was fed by her wonderful inner glow.

The same thing is true of the problems of movement. Gone would be the unrelated slouch, the self-conscious hands in the pockets, the sawing of the air, the running of the fingers through the hair of so many Method advocates if they really were following Stanislavski and that right side of the column on his chart. Anton Chekhov, the writer, who was the realists' god and the Stanislavski-methodists' first great author, said, "When a man spends the least possible number of movements over some definite action. that is grace."

Finally, I would add that the technique of producing emotion should be related to the whole problem of acting and the complete demands of the play, and not become a fetish used for its own sake. If that were so we would have the actor stretching himself up to the level of art and not pulling all art down to the comfortable level of his "real-life" truth. We would also have more beautiful, considerate feeling and less "squeezed-out," self-centered emotion.

Good-bye till next Monday night.

MAY 13, 1957

"TRUTH" IN ACTING

What is truth? Now this is a hot subject. Naturally, I mean what is truth in acting. If you remember, when I promised in the first talk to get to this point, I said I felt there were more crimes committed, artistically speaking, in the name of truth than in the name of any other virtue. I also said I would ask the question as to whether or not the point (of the Method) was to reproduce our "real life" on the stage, and who wants it? Had not Stanislavski himself said, "An authentic 'fact,' and genuine reality do not exist on the stage! Reality is not art. This last, by its very nature, needs artistic invention, which means first of all the work of an author. The actor's task and his creative technique consist in transforming the invented play into *artistic* and *scenic* fact!"

Of course there is no denying that the aim of the Stanislavski Method was to encourage more truthful acting. What started his study was the posturing and false imitating he saw in the actors of his day; he felt there must be some way in which one could use one's own sense of truth to create parts. But now it comes down to the question

87

of *what* truth? Is it to be the truth that represents the comfort of the particular actor involved; that is, the truth nearest to his own particular psychology? Is that all that is meant by it? If so, isn't that truth just a *partial* truth? And how true is a partial truth in life? Are we to be comfortable, true-feeling actors or are we to be artists who use our true feelings as one of the tools of our craft to create with?

The first problem in discussing this subject is to overcome the difficulty of defining the word truth at all. The same words, in art, mean different things to different people. For instance: I know an actress, a charming, sincere, witty, intelligent person who, whenever you meet her, speaks with openness, sincerity, wit, intelligence, forthrightness and directness; but she does not act very well. It always bothered me because I could not understand why somebody who is so direct and sincere in life suddenly got so artificial when she walked onstage. One day I thought I would try to see if I could get the answer. I spoke to her about this and that and finally got around to her acting problem. She explained, "Oh, well, life is one thing, what with talking and kidding around and expressing myself, but when I go on the *stage*," and here her voice took on a respectful, but sepulchral tone, "then I have to be *sincere!*" To her, sincerity was that special *thing* she added in that was her art. It was destroying her as an actress. Can one say to her, "Then please be as phony onstage as you are in life?"

I remember, too, in the very first show I directed on Broadway, *My Heart's in the Highlands*, one of the morning papers said that the performance was "in the best *realistic* tradition of Stanislavski's Moscow Art Theatre," while an afternoon paper said it was *"cubist!"*

The same confusion goes on about truth in acting. People in all categories, public as well as professional, are sometimes easily fooled. Falseness often moves them; truth is often resented. It is an agonizing situation for an artist. People are moved by falseness, I suppose, because they bring their own sense of truth to it and read into the falseness what they wish to know. All they need is the *key* for them to feel; it does not have to be done for them. They need only to be *reminded* of their own true feeling about the situation. Then, too, real truth can be resented because it makes people feel uncomfortable. And, because they are uncomfortable, they say it is not true. Now these are only partial answers; but they are something we have to deal with and think about.

To come back to the actors: are the "one hundred percent living-the-part" actors really living the *part* one hundred per-cent, or are they just living *themselves* one hundred per-cent and adding the author's words to their own life onstage? More, are they not often even paraphrasing the author's words although they themselves can't even write letters to their mothers? Must every "yes" be a "yeah" —even if it is not a "yeah"-type character? Is this not done solely for comfort? And is it not a comment that "yeah" is more comfortable than "yes"? "Yeah" would have been very *un*comfortable for John Barrymore. Is "yeah" more manly than "yes"? John Barrymore was a man. I sometimes wonder whether the "yeah"-sayers are really more manly than John Barrymore. At best it's a phony concept.

89

You constantly hear, in rehearsal, "I don't feel it." In variations it goes, "I don't feel it that way" or, "I don't feel it if he's going to do that." When I hear that I want to say, "Who cares? It's the *audience* which is supposed to feel it!" I think it is an excuse for the fact that the actor is not *doing* what he should be doing. I think if he really *does* it right, he will feel it! Or, if not, we must find out what he is doing that is wrong. It is a mistake to wait to act until you feel. I think that you must act and feeling will come; but in the meantime you must act. (Talk, listen, execute your proper intention, etc. etc.)

A time that I was most moved in the theatre had nothing to do with this Method and its inner feeling. This was when I saw the great Chinese actor, Mei Lan-fang, perform. Corny as it may sound, when I left the theatre I walked around for two hours before I could go home. I didn't even notice that it was drizzling. Now he didn't "feel," psychologically speaking, at all. When he was supposed to be crying he took his fan, put it in a certain position which just revealed his eyes and made a mewing sound, rhythmic, beautiful. That was to let us know he was crying. All of his conventions, his whole *method*, served to demonstrate for us the emotions he was supposed to be feeling through this technique, his art, which consisted of many things: movement, sound, dance, music. So, too, he let us know what *we* were to feel, and he did it in such a beautiful and imaginative way that it inspired the highest feelings in us. He not only aroused in us the feeling of appreciation for beauty but he moved us in any way he wanted us to be moved. There was one scene where he committed suicide on the stage. He played the part of a young girl and, in this scene, wore his wig and a white kimono. What he did was to undo the wig, take a strand of hair from either side and put them through his mouth thus making a cross. He then took a large curved sword and held it at his throat. Standing in place, he suddenly started to twirl with that sword at his head. To give the impression of cutting his head off he twirled round and round and round and suddenly stopped absolutely dead still. His head fell a little to one side, his eyes crossed, then he held there and the curtain came down. We really felt that the head was severed from the body, that he *had* cut his head off. I don't know how one could act that "with feeling" to inspire more terror in the audience. We couldn't applaud, we couldn't do anything. We were terrified! Certainly, the audience should also, then, share the truly-experienced emotions of our realistic actors.

Now isn't this emphasis on self-indulgent feeling the result of a false concept of "psychological truth," which may mean the actor's psychology and not the truth of art at all (because the elements of art are not present)? All is brought to one's own understanding of the moment, to one's own level. It is not the author's, or even the character's, thinking, but the actor's own. This happens often even in the plays of realistic modern authors. All of their thoughts and ideas are brought to the particular psychological concept of the actor involved. What happens when we reach Shakespeare's realm?

This "leveling" effect is not too far removed from what occurs, on another plane, when you go to Hollywood and have a story conference. Somebody says, "So here the dame enters and she claps her eye on the guy and we're off to the races!" With this reducing of all situations to their lowest denominator, it is true that *Romeo and Juliet* does in fact become *Abie's Irish Rose!* It *is* the same story if you are just going to say it's about a guy and a girl and their two families who fight. So too, if just your personal feeling is emphasized, does it not account for the frequent charge of "sameness" in Method actors? Truthfully, have not some of us studied the whole first half of the chart to the detriment of the second half? (Or to put it another way: *An Actor Prepares* to the detriment of *Creating a Character?*) Why? I keep thinking about it all the time because I've been reading to you out of that second book for several weeks now and it denies everything that people complain about in the Method. Maybe the publication dates of the two books have something to do with it. One was published thirteen years after the other, as we know, and it may be that, by that time, it was too late. Then again perhaps it wouldn't have mattered; it may be just laziness in technique, self-indulgence and personality problems.

For example: Is fixing a distorted line-reading phony? I am a practicing director. I direct something every year and I am constantly faced with somebody saying, "Please don't tell me how to read it. Don't give me the line reading, it will make me phony." All in the name of Stanislavski's bible and a desire for "truth" the actor says, "Please, I want to feel the thing right and if you are going to give me a specific line reading it will just be a mechanical thing!" Yet again and again my problem as a director has been that this moment of the play is not clear simply because the line is being read wrong! So I open this book,

Building a Character, again where Stanislavski says, "Logical pauses unite words into groups (or speech measures) and they divide the groups from one another. Do you realize that a man's fate, and even his very life may depend on the position of that pause? Take the words: 'Pardon impossible send to Siberia.' How can we understand the meaning of this order until we know where the logical pause is placed? Put them in and the sense of the words will become clear. Either you say: 'Pardon—impossible send to Siberia,' or 'Pardon impossible—send to Siberia!' In the first it is a case for mercy, in the second, exile."

Now some purist actors feel that if they have to think of things like accenting the right word they can't act. They say acting is something that is generated inside them and can't be subjected to such controls. I say to you, isn't that theory just as phony as the actor who says, "If I have to think of my intentions as well as my lines, it's as if I were playing two parts"? You may laugh all you want but a very well-known and successful actor said that to me when I told him what he was supposed to be thinking as he said a certain line. "That's impossible," he said. "Just give me the line reading! I'll do it any way you say. Just read it for me. But don't tell me what I'm supposed to be thinking because that's as if I had to play two parts at once and I just can't do it!"

In this case, the famous actor was using his concentration and energy for the least important purpose in acting, which was in remembering his lines and their inflections. But in our earlier example, the sole emphasis on blind feeling has bound the actor and made him helpless in every

93

other way. He may feel that moment correctly but he is hitting the wrong word every time and thus changing the point. And, if he *has* to do that, I think it is just as phony.

By the way, speaking of phoniness, I think there is nothing as phony as the prevalent fear of being phony (on the stage). It comes from the avoidance of certain other truths; truths which are the very foundations of the artist. For example, the appreciation of form.

There is even no reason why you can't retain your actor's sense of truth while having to read for a part. There is sometimes no other way of finding out whether someone whose work you don't know has the right quality for a certain rôle. You can tell a good deal by an interview, but a reading might reveal something you can't be sure of just by meeting the actor. It is possible to pick up a part and, without extensive preparation, give an adequate reading. Sometimes, even, a first reading can be startlingly good. But, at worst, you can simply *talk* and *listen.* The director, if he's present, may give you a few hints to help. Although auditioning is never an ideal situation in our theatre, an intelligent actor can give some inkling of what is needed to be known by not forcing feelings he doesn't have and by not trying to accomplish the whole characterization in the audition. Something of his potential in the part is bound to be uncovered. Of course, it goes without saying that the people listening to the audition must be intelligent, too, and not expect a finished performance.

For a moment let's talk about our truthful emotion and how to work for it on a part. Now I certainly agree with Stanislavski when he says that of the three motors—the mind, the will and the heart—that generate our actors' en-

94

ergy and make us perform, the heart is the most capricious. But I have found that if you use the *mind*, which includes the understanding of the whole play, the situations and the characters, and if with your *will* (if you are really talking and listening) you fully execute exciting intentions, then the proper *emotion* should be present. Now it is quite possible you'll say, "It just isn't present," or "What's present is not enough!" If that does happen, first try further stimulation from the first two processes without getting into a panic about the feeling end of it, and go in for some deeper therapy. Let's first try to cure it without straying from the play itself. Let us say that in this moment the intention you have worked out is not strong enough to stimulate your feelings; then change it. Instead of "to prevent him from saying that," make it "to tear his tongue out if he says it!" You are still in a realm that you can control: you are still using your mind to give you an idea; and you are still using your will to execute that idea. You will find, if you go about it in that way, that most of the time you will get the desired feeling.

If it is something even deeper that you need, something more subtle, then you also have the "as if" phrase. You can say to yourself, "What is it *like*? What is the *nature* of this moment? What more can I understand by it since it itself doesn't seem to generate my motor emotionally?" I have this problem all the time as a director, too. When I read a certain play I was to direct I came to a point where a character had to face somebody that she had loved, after an absence, and now she had to castigate him because of something horrendous she believed he had done. When I came to that point in the play I was extremely moved be-

95

cause it touched something in my own life. I had been in that situation once. I knew it was going to be a difficult moment for the actress because it just so happened that there was not much preparation for it in the scene. I said to her, "I don't know what you are going to do in this moment. You are on the stage, it happens quickly and there you are faced with it. It should be a terribly moving moment for you. All I can do is to tell you what moved me about it." I told her my story and the actress said, "I know just what you mean, because that same thing happened to me. It was in an entirely different way, but I understand that feeling. I've been faced with a similar situation." I never asked her what it was. Her feeling was always right at this point in the play. She deeply understood something comparable to the situation in the story and used this personal experience in her part.

Now this approach toward the problem of "affective memory" seems to me to be normal because it is related to the situation in the play.

This business of true feeling is not just this year's discussion—it just has taken a peculiar turn lately. I always try to keep in mind the date of articles on the subject. That is very important because modern acting, just like modern life, has been very much affected by the research in psychology that has gone on in recent years. A good deal of our problem now stems from the fact that we have learned a lot about reflexes and the like which did not enter into the earlier arguments. The discussion of the basic artistic principle of real vs. simulated feeling, however, has been going on for some time; it's just that our language about it has now become a little different. We can't turn the clock back; we have all this new scientific material to deal with and we have to incorporate it somehow into our understanding and our work.

Now, to pursue this a little further, M. Louis Jouvet said, in an article, that on the stage the actor should hide what he feels and show what he doesn't. I was stumped by this for some time. I tried very hard to understand it. I thought to myself, "Now let me see. 'The actor should hide what he feels and show what he doesn't.' Now why should you *hide* and not *use* what you feel? And conversely, won't showing what you *don't* feel make for empty posturing?" Then one day I read that Jouvet had also said, "Be the character and feel *his* feelings," and suddenly the first puzzling statement became clear.

I saw that possibly there was a good meaning in his remark; that what he probably meant was that the actor should conceal his *personal* feeling and create the feeling needed by the author and the character. But, at any rate, since you use your own heart as the *material* of emotion, I think the Jouvet statement becomes too cryptic. Besides, it contains two negatives.

Now Stanislavski's approach to truth stemmed from the writer, Pushkin, of whom he was very fond. The Moscow Art Theatre, by the way, did all the classics. They did not do just realistic plays. They did Shakespeare, Goldoni, etc. At any rate, as we know from his chart, Stanislavski quoted Pushkin, who, in a letter answering a question about writing, said, "The truth of passion, the verisimilitude of feeling, placed in the given circumstances, that is what our reason demands of a writer or of a dramatic poet." And Stanislavski took that to refer to acting as well.

97

I'll repeat it because it is a really remarkable sentence. "The truth of passion, the verisimilitude of feeling, placed in the given circumstances, that is what our reason demands of a writer or of a dramatic poet." Now the phrase I wish to extract momentarily from that statement for you is, "placed in the given circumstances." Given circumstances do not only mean, for example, that a taxi is waiting for you outside and therefore you have to hurry through the scene. That is a given circumstance when you come on, that is true. But that is only one application of the term. I would hope that he meant: given *all* the circumstances of the particular play—which might be, for example, that the characters do not live in the Bronx, they live in 17th Century France; that the author of the play has written it in a certain style which must find its counterpart in the performance, etc.

We might try to define for ourselves some approaches to truth in acting:

One: the kind of "indicated" truth, the imitation of feeling, the falsely-effective acting that just needs nerve to accomplish. (Not preferred by me, incidentally.) It is true that it may satisfy some, but it goes no deeper into our experience than cheesy writing does (which can also affect you), or empty, "posy" dancing, which doesn't spring from any inner impulse.

Two: (still not preferable, for my taste) the kind of personalized feeling which may be really felt, but is unconnected with the source of the material being interpreted and brings all to the particular level of the actor, which may not always be high enough. (This, incidentally, seems to me the reverse of what used to happen with Duse, the

Scene from William Saroyan's *My Heart's in the Highlands*, as directed by Mr. Lewis.

realists' goddess, who elevated commonplace plays with her artistry. She seldom played in really good plays. But she brought her own sense of art to them and created ideas which were unforgettable and which lived beyond the life of the material itself.) This second approach, the exploitation of personal feeling, implies that one can tackle the Ninth Symphony of Beethoven with the same "feeling of truth" with which you tackle Offenbach's Gaité Parisienne!

Now there is a third approach (which *is* preferable to me). It is the truth that is really experienced, but artistically controlled, and correctly used for the particular character portrayed, the complete circumstances of the scene, and the chosen style of the author and play being performed.

I think we can do without the "beautiful," possibly "effective," sympathy-begging, exterior acting *and* the "ugly," personally-experienced, unadjusted to artistic requirements, interior-feeling, bottom-scratching Hamlets! I saw a performance of *The Merchant of Venice* in which a fairly well-known actress playing *Portia* tried to make her part "real." With all the best will in the world she came out and said, quite casually, "The quality of mercy *isn't* strained! It droppeth—asthegentlerainfromheavenupontheplaceb e n e a t h. It is twice blessed! [*And here she counted off on two fingers.*] It blesseth him that GIVES and him that TAKES!" Oh, it was very real. But it was *her* reality, not Shakespeare's.

Yes, I think we can safely reject that first group who do all their empty, "beautiful" acting in the name of theatricality and the second group who do all their monotonous, strained acting in the name of truth. This is the point

I am trying to bring into focus gradually, week by week. I don't think that truth need be untheatrical or that theatricality need be false. It is not advisable to use only outside means to create, because I do believe that stifles your true feeling instead of releasing it; but you can start your inside motor up and keep it running to create your means of projecting the whole truth of your part in a play. You might say it is something like a sound heart in a sound body.

As there is choice always in all elements of art, so too I think there must be choice in emotion if we are to have real truth. Here I refer not only to choice in relation to style, but even to choice within the realistic form itself. The depth of feeling of one character is different from another, and if you are always feeling truthfully as *you* feel, you may hit your character only intermittently, if at all. If a certain character is supposed to say, unappreciatively and jokingly, "You know, when I hear Wagner's music I just get nervous," and the actor comes on stage and solemnizes the line, the author has a perfect right to come running down the aisle and shout, "Wait a minute! That was supposed to be funny! You are giving me *your* feeling about Wagner and I don't give a damn about your feeling! I want the *character's* feeling about Wagner, and he doesn't even know who or what Wagner is!"

Now part of the reason for this tendency may be the danger I mentioned last week of continuously working on "big" scenes in workshops, making all simple problems seem to be unimportant. Yet each and every problem in the part added up is what makes the rôle—not only the big moments. But mainly, I think, it is the self-indulgent attitude of actors who want to feel "good," and, because of that, gravitate naturally to feelings that are closest to them and therefore more comfortable for them. It is unlike the artist who studies his material and chooses his elements correctly to create with. And I want to tell you the artist's way of working is very often agonizing and not at all comfortable. The whole, all-too-prevalent idea of the limiting of emotion to the natural, easy, daily responses of the actor to situations is stultifying to the imagination, which is the most powerful weapon of the artist. We have already had the example of Michael Chekhov in *The Deluge*, who when he felt he had to let his partner know he really loved him in spite of the way he had fought with him, began digging at his partner's heart, trying to get inside and become one with him—that is imagination! You always hear the example of Duse in *Ghosts*. When she stood at the door watching her son with the maid and realizing it was the father all over again, she had to say the word, "Ghosts!" At the moment she said it she struck out with her fists as if she were trying to fight these ghosts off—imagination! Grasso, the great Sicilian actor, played a painter, in a play, who had a young apprentice whom he taught and loved; and one day he came home to find the young boy making love to Grasso's wife. Grasso was a big, powerful man and he started toward the boy to kill him; the boy was so terrified he couldn't move but just stood there. Grasso came closer and closer and when he reached the boy he unexpectedly grabbed him and hugged him. Grasso hadn't read Freud but he knew, as an artist, that somewhere in there the reason he wanted to kill the boy was not hatred for stealing his wife but because his

101

own love and trust of the boy had been betrayed. Imagination!

Now you may say that in the first case what Michael Chekhov was doing was employing "psychological gesture." In the second case you can maintain that Duse was "playing her objective" which was to fight off those ghosts of the past. You may feel that Grasso was "playing the opposite." But I say to you that you can call any one of the things spinach as far as I'm concerned because they all could have played those moments truthfully with full feeling and still not reached the peaks they did. In the first case Chekhov could have played the scene marvellously well without that digging gesture and it still would have been "full;" Duse could have just stood there absolutely filled with the feeling of fear that her husband's sins were coming back and the ghosts of the past were attacking her again—she did not need to strike out at those ghosts—and it still would have been a good emotional moment; Grasso, with that great swell of feeling he had, could have gone right to the boy and shaken the daylights out of him and it would have been absolutely true, too. But if these actors had been content merely with feeling truthfully I tell you we would not be here talking about any of them today. Because imagination *is* the reality of the artist! Imagination is the material that artists work with. Truth must not be made into a static, stultifying thing. In art, truth should be the search for truth.

MAY 20, 1957

ACTORS OR ARTISTS?

Do too many students of the Stanislavski Method use it for the development of certain aspects of acting rather than for understanding and growth of artistry?

Actor or artist? I looked both up in the dictionary and under "actor" it said, "theatrical performer; a stage player; a performer in motion pictures." I presume the next edition of Webster's will add—a performer in TV. I then looked up "artist" and it said, "one who professes and practices an art in which conception and execution are governed by imagination and taste." As far as we are here concerned, in a definition of an artist, I would like to add (after conceding the sense of truth which I think we've belabored enough) the following three aspects. First, a sense of the whole—as a painter sees the whole picture in his mind's eye as he paints. I have a feeling that even certain modernists in painting, who may just start from anywhere on the canvas and let their luck take them where it will, must be guided by some subconscious sense of the whole which emerges at the end.

Actors are often inclined to become specialists with no

sense of the whole. They become specialists in feeling their own part truthfully to the exclusion of all of the other elements that make up good theatre. Actors, of course, are not the only specialists in the theatre. If you have ever been to a road tryout of a musical where there are costumers, scenery designers, composers, choreographers, lyricists, book writers and so forth, all working on the show, you must have noticed the traffic in the theatre lobby every night during the performance. As the ballet is about to begin the book writer flies out to get a cigarette and the choreographer rushes in to see his ballet, and so on. I suppose the director is the one person who has to sit there through it all. I'm fond of telling a story about the costume designer of *Brigadoon,* which I directed. The show had played New Haven and we then went on to Boston to open on Monday night. With very little time to set up we were terrified that things were not going to go well technically. The curtain went up on the first set, a small scene of two fellows lost in a forest, and it went along all right. The curtain came down on that scene and then there was a walk-over scene in front of the curtain in which the "merry villagers" come on waking up after having been asleep for a hundred years. As they came across the stage, the crew was setting up the next big scene behind the curtain, which was the village of MacConnachy Square. The orchestra was playing while the villagers sang as they went across the stage. It was a continuous scene; as they sang, "Come ye everywhere, to the fair," the curtain was supposed to go up and these people in front then blended with the crowd behind the curtain who were dancing and singing up a storm. But this night when, "Come

106

ye everywhere, to the fair" came, the curtain did not go up; it just stayed there. It was a terrifying moment! I was standing in the back and I grabbed choreographer Agnes DeMille's arm, breaking it only slightly. The conductor couldn't stop the orchestra because it was a continuous scene; the people behind the curtain were already singing —you could hear them clearly. Still it didn't go up. Then, slowly, the people behind gradually got discouraged and their voices began to fade away. Now, of the people in front, those who were near either side, just sneaked off; those in the center had too far to go—they were trapped. Then finally, after an eternity, with the number half over, the curtain went up with a jerk. A few of the chorus were still singing and dancing a little, some were just standing around, still others were seated on the floor—the whole thing looked like the Edinburgh subway! In addition, at the same time that the front curtain went up the backdrop, on which the village of MacConnachy Square was painted, went up too, revealing the back wall of the Colonial Theatre in Boston. It was at this moment that the costume designer rushed up to me, grabbed my arm and said, "That chorus girl has the wrong socks on again!" Now *that* is specialization!

Secondly, I think it is important for us, as artists, to have a sense of style. I'm going to skip over that for the moment because we will cover it next week when we come to the Method in relation to poetic drama, Shakespeare, musicals, etc.

But the third aspect of the artist, and the one I want to tackle tonight, is the sense of form: the build-up of the parts that make the whole, the dynamics that govern them, and the controls that keep the form constant. Acting, with its dependence on the human quotients—the mind, heart and will, all functioning in the instrument itself which is the human body—is apt to be less constant than sculpture, for instance, which can be finished forever once it is done. I feel this only means that a closer attention to controls is indicated.

Then there is the sense of balance in the problem of form. All the great artists I've witnessed in any field have had this sense of balance. They were great equalizers. They saw all around a problem, not just one side of it. I am reminded of the great dancer, Argentina. Though a very fine Spanish dancer, she was really important beyond that insofar as she brought to everything she danced this wonderful equalizing sense. When she danced her number about the Queen in the Spanish Court there was something slightly awkward and clumsy about it; when she did her famous dance about the fisher-girl, a peasant number, she behaved with all the dignity of a queen.

In the same Casals book that I referred to before,* he said that "one cannot undertake the performance of a great work without first sorting out its principal trends, its architectural sense, and the relation between the different elements which make up its structure." In reference to writing, Thomas Carlyle gave us one of the most beautiful statements: "It is meritorious to insist on forms. Religion and all else naturally clothes itself in forms. All substances clothe themselves in forms; but there are suitable true forms, and then there are untrue unsuitable. As the briefest definition one might say, Forms which *grow* round a

* *Conversations with Casals.*

108

substance, if we rightly understand that, will correspond to the real Nature and purport of it, will be true, good; forms which are consciously *put* round a substance, bad. I invite you to reflect on this. It distinguishes true from false in Ceremonial Form, earnest solemnity from empty pageant, in all human beings."

I think there is a mistaken conception that form is a problem for Molière, or some such "stylized" plays, but that in the realistic theatre we are recreating life and are less concerned with form. I contend that realism itself is a form, one of the theatrical forms, and that all art, *even photography,* has form. Alfred Stieglitz, who is considered by many to be one of the greatest photographers who ever lived, when he could not put his hands on the actual objects (clouds or buildings) to compose them into the picture he wished to photograph, sat around and waited until they formed themselves into what he wanted. He took his famous picture of the office building in Manhattan from his gallery at 509 Madison Avenue. He looked out of the window and saw something in that tall building that he wanted to photograph. What he obviously saw in it is what the picture shows—a great structure which has a curious air of emptiness. There are lights on all over but not a sign of life in the building. He had to wait an awfully long time; he waited hour after hour by that window, night after night, until just the right second came which gave the building that look which the artist envisioned.

What is the form of realistic theatre? We ought to be able to put our finger on it. Stanislavski, the god of so many formless ones, had, as we have seen, a word or two to pinpoint it. Take, for comparison, the symphony in music. The movements in a symphony correspond to the acts in a play. The themes of a symphony, the main theme and then the subordinate themes, can be compared to the "spine" and the "intentions" in that chart of the Method we looked at. The general tempo-mark at the beginning of a musical piece (allegro, grave, etc.) is comparable to the "long-distance mood" of Stanislavski's, the pervading mood that goes through a whole play. Certainly, in the "Eroica" symphony, the idea of it being a kind of tribute to nobility, heroism, is the thing that gives the whole piece its mood. For example, there is a funeral march movement in it. Well, there are funeral marches in other works, but this one has to be played with a heroic tone because the mood of the whole symphony has been set down by the composer. The same principle is true in a play. Further, the dynamic marks throughout a musical score correspond to our timing, pauses, etc.

We also have scores, as in music. Of course, everybody knows about the director's score, the regisseur's book, which has all his staging markings and his production plan in it. The actor also can, and I think should, have his score. All during rehearsal I keep saying, "Write your intentions down!" But no one ever brings a pencil. We then give out pencils. I say, "I know you remember them now, but you won't later. They will slip away. Write them down! You have your part with the dialogue on the right-hand page. There is no reason not to put down your corresponding intentions on that beautiful blank page on the left." I think if you will mark down all your acting ideas as you work them out in rehearsal with your director it will help you to retain the form of your performance. It will also assist you in keeping up your performance. When it starts to slip you very often don't notice where you have changed one tiny little thing, but the scene is not "playing" any more. It's not making its impact and you don't know what has happened. Well, you should have your score. You, the actor, ought to be able to go back to your score and look at the "dynamic markings" of that scene and see what it is that you are now not doing. If, for example, you find that the specific line where it was decided you should "start to suspect him" is actually three lines before you challenge him (in the dialogue) and you have been suspecting him on the challenging line, then you might know the reason why the audience has been coughing on those three lines these last few performances. You are not starting to suspect him in the right place any more. You are not doing it until you face him three lines later. That little bit has somehow slipped out of your performance. And it is this successful scene-by-scene fulfillment of the intentions which is the essence of the realistic form of theatre.

In case you think I am just talking about the Group Theatre or something comparable, I have a quote about a great English actress, Edith Evans, on this very point, "Her plan is thorough. Before rehearsing any new part, she writes another, and an unspoken part between the lines so that every night she can think as the character would." It is obvious that she studies both the words and her subtext together.

I would now like to demonstrate how the sense of form manifests itself in an actual production from the point of view of the director and the actors. I went through my directing scripts and picked out *The Teahouse of the*

August Moon because I thought probably most of you would have seen that and would remember the moments I am going to speak about. That might keep this from being merely theoretic.

Keep in mind now that we are starting from the sense of the whole and working right down to the specific moments I will pick out of the play. I first said to myself, "What is it about? What is the theme?—Well, obviously it's about the following: that to 'occupy,' or force your culture onto, anyone, is silly—you might get occupied yourself." And I wrote it down that way, exactly that way. Because the play was funny, I used the word "silly." Words you choose are very important when you work. I could have said, "that to 'occupy,' or force your culture onto, anyone, is terrible!" It would be virtually the same idea but the play was a comedy and it would immediately have started me to thinking along another line instead of all the funny ways in which the idea could be dramatized. Then I said, "It looks to me as if, to bring out this point, there are two lines that develop and cross in the course of the evening: one is, that the Americans get more and more orientalized (they start out in their G.I. clothes and end up with sandals and bathrobes, performing tea ceremonies); the other, that the Orientals become partially Americanized (Sakini's speaking American slang, the townspeople starting a business enterprise, their singing of *Deep in the Heart of Texas*)." Now I had to bring out this theme first through all of the theatre elements that would be on the stage. The sets, for example, had to tell that story in their way. They could have just been serviceable or pretty, but then they would not be demonstrating

112

this theme. So we started from the Quonset huts and gradually orientalized them. In the next set we had a bit of an oriental arch which was made of the tail end of a wrecked American plane supported on one side by a bamboo pole. Now we could have had just a plain, nice oriental arch which would have served the purpose, but it would not have told this particular story, which was that when this plane had cracked up, the natives had used the remains, and supported it with a bamboo pole. This idea was gradually going to be demonstrated in a deeper sense in the play.

Costumes followed the same pattern. The G.I.'s clothes gradually developed into bathrobes, straw hats, and wooden sandals; and the young native artist who started out in his oriental clothes ended up with a U.S. sailor shirt.

Now I want to get to the acting which is what we are concerned with. I said to each actor, "If it is so that the whole play has to do with how everybody solves this problem of occupation, what are you doing in relation to that main theme?" To *Sakini* I said, "Well, under this occupation what you do is to manage the whole show." Now he had a double job because he managed the whole show in the actual theatre as well as managing the whole show of the occupation. I said, "*Sakini* is two characters in one—he is the one who comes out in front and speaks to the audience and the fellow who plays in the play. The first character should be more or less as he himself is, and the second one should be as he thinks the Americans like to see him. He has a bit of "Uncle Tomishness" in him, especially with *Colonel Purdy* or when he is teasing *Fisby*, plus a bit of Groucho Marx, and he is a great mimic." This

113

may seem silly now but any single suggestion that you get may make the whole part clear for you. I acted in a movie once with Charlie Chaplin, a great director. He just said one thing to me about the part I played (a little druggist who prepared a perfect poison for him in *Monsieur Verdoux*) that struck home. He said, "When this fellow speaks, he doesn't talk to you—he lectures to you." That was all he needed to say. It immediately gave me the whole way of thinking, of speaking, of enjoying the big words that I had to say, etc. It even suggested my whole make-up.

I'm not going to go through the main objectives of the rest of the parts in *Teahouse*. I just wanted to show you again that, once you have the theme of the play, you take each character and attach him to that main idea so all the parts will hold together on that single axle.

Now what happens when you start to break down the scenes? What does the actor put on that blank left-hand page that will keep the form of his part? To answer, I will analyze the beginning of the play for you. It is a monologue, the first monologue of *Sakini*.

I said to the actor, "The first thing you have to do at the curtain is to introduce *Sakini's* two characters so that the audience understands at once that you are to play this double part. They will then be able to follow that idea through the play." To do that we first had him run across the apron as if he were still preparing the show backstage and on his way to tell something to the electrician when, suddenly, half-way across, he noticed that the audience in the theatre had already gathered. Although surprised, he pulled himself together and then bowed, very formally, three times, which is the oriental convention. So we saw

114

Scene from *The Teahouse of the August Moon*, as directed by Mr. Lewis

that he was not a formal fellow but was acting that aspect of it. In that very first move, before he said a single word, the two characters were introduced. After the formal bows were over, he lapsed back into his informal GI pose, studied the customers, and chewed gum to show that he was a "real GI."

The next thing for *Sakini* to do was his stage-managing job. In the Japanese Kabuki theatre there is a fellow, called the Kurogo, who is a sort of prompter and stage-manager. He is dressed in black and runs around doing everything that needs to be done in full view of the audience. I said, "The first thing you have to do is *to introduce yourself.*" The line was "*Sakini* by name." "Now," I said, "put a stroke in your part after the first word in the next four lines. In other words, don't say, '*Sakini* by name' but say '*Sakini/* (pause) by name, Interpreter/ by profession,' and so on down through the fourth line because the last line of that sequence is, 'Okinawan/ by whim of gods.' The idea being —about *that* I could do nothing!"

Now I mention the rhythm of that sequence of lines as an example of what we have been talking about in relation to truth. *Sakini* could have been just as truthful saying, "*Sakini* by name, Interpreter by profession," without those slight pauses, and introduced himself quite adequately. But this way he had a rhythmic pattern which not only gave the monologue a sense of poetry, but also built to a laugh, if you'll pardon the expression!

Next, *Sakini* says, "History of Okinawa, etc." and that section I said was "to give the exciting background of the story." Now you may say there is no need to write that down because the line says that—it says, "History of Oki-

115

nawa." But the reason why you should put it down is because if you know that at that point you are doing something new and *exciting*, you start there with a fresh impulse. Otherwise, this monologue might drone on forever. But, if it is broken up into clear sections in which you have downbeats, etc., as in music, you then have the rhythm and dynamics which create an artistic pattern.

I give this example from *Teahouse* to show that there is nothing incompatible with a sense of form in the ideas inherent in the principles of Stanislavski. Quite the contrary. They can, and should, be used for the creation and preservation of form in acting as well as directing. It is time we looked not to the Master, but to the disciples, for the answer to charges of formlessness.

Now, with this sense of form there is a certain amount of human play that is present in the realistic theatre. Actors, we have said, are people with hearts, minds and wills and they are using these as well as their voices, gestures, walks, etc. And, since they are bringing themselves onto the stage to create in a certain place at a certain time, they are subject to these human laws. As a result, it is quite possible that there is, and will be, more or less feeling in a given performance. Salvini played *Othello* a hundred times in his whole life, and he lived to be an old man, but he said he only *really* played it about two or three times in all that time. He meant he fully experienced the whole part, with all the inner and outer controls, only a few times. So how do you expect, with our long-run system, that a performance is always going to be full just to the proper degree and not go over or under a little. It is not possible. But, I repeat, the things that can keep the sense of the play going, and which does hold the form together, are those fully-executed intentions.

I saw *The Glass Menagerie* three times and I would say that Laurette Taylor was never *exactly* the same. And yet, for our purposes, I would say that she *was* always the same because her sense of form was constant. Her understanding of the woman was complete, her understanding of the play was complete, exactly who all these other people were that she was talking to was fully understood at all times, and what she had to accomplish in each scene was eminently clear to her. Now she may have varied a little in this place or that. Sometimes she was a little funnier here or there, and sometimes she was a little more moved than at another time. But she always understood the whole intent of the scene, and in that sense the *form* was constant.

To sum up, the form of a performance lies in the successful scene-by-scene fulfillment of the main intention of each character in relation to the theme of the play. While attention must be paid, even in a realistic production, to all the physical means of expressing this inner content, the special problems of Style will be taken up next week.

[*Question from the audience*]: Do you as a director look for Method actors in casting? [*Answer*]: Well, I can answer the question very quickly. I think the theatre uses everything, and if the person is good for the part and can do it that's fine by me. I don't care about anything else at all. As a working director I say that categorically. But there is a question within this question which ought to be answered because I think there is a certain misconception

117

about casting. And a great deal of trouble arises out of this in production.

What you ought to look for in choosing someone for a part is whether or not that person can play, and is right for, the highest moment in the part, regardless of whether he exactly fits the first entrance or not. I have seen more parts misinterpreted and more plays destroyed because the casting was done from the description of the characters at the beginning of the play. That description usually reads something like, "Enter Ruth. She is a lovely young girl of fine proportions with blond hair and a cute curl in her upper lip. She is dressed in a fine spring frock which she wears with a jaunty air." So you find a girl like that and give her the part because she answers the description perfectly. Now she comes on in the first scene, says, "Joe, darling, how are you?", is enchanting, everything goes along fine and she gets a big hand at the end of the scene. Then comes the end of the second act and it turns out that dear Ruth is a born murderess! But nobody believes it! The audience has to be convinced that this girl would kill Joe for a nickel but you have chosen Mary Miles Minter to play the part! . . . It happens every day. The price that's paid for this casting misconception is enormous! The playwrights ought to catch on too because they often wonder, "What happened to my play? It's not getting over!" You see, the actors are getting big hands because they have already made their marks in the opening scenes, and when the play suddenly seems boring, nobody is going to blame all those fine actors who did everything so well in the first act, yet something seems to be wrong. It must be the play!

118

You should look for the *essential* quality of the part in casting the person to play it. This is aside from physical things. What really is going to tell the story? If any of you are old enough to have seen Jeanne Eagels in *Rain,* you will remember that the thing that made it wonderful was that the essential quality of the actress was a certain inner purity. Jeanne Eagels had pink cheeks, the prettiest face you ever saw, and a desire to be good. Now then, with all of that, she dressed up like Sadie Thompson and when she came on you said, "But that's a basically good girl!" And when she had the scene with the minister who spoke in religious platitudes, you said, "He shouldn't be talking that way to this lovely girl!" I've seen that play many times since and they have always cast a girl who, when she came out in the beginning, was obviously closer to the cliché of a Sadie Thompson. It then seems like a corny melodrama, but it wasn't with Jeanne Eagels—it was very moving.

There is another point, to finish this casting question, and that is the whole problem of stage beauty. There are certain faces that are beautiful in life which don't mean a darned thing on the stage. There are other faces which have a certain luminousness on the stage which, upon close examination, may not contain the features of the ideal beauty. The thing that seems beautiful on the stage is what emanates from a person who has a beautiful quality, understanding, charm, wit, mind, feeling. You can put the prettiest person in the world on the stage and if she doesn't have some of those qualities, she not only does not give the impression of beauty but actually does not even look beautiful. I've seen that happen. Their faces fade

119

away like the Cheshire cat; after a while you hardly see them at all. Beauty on the stage is something which is created, moment by moment; it is not only a physical thing.

Finally, it is the sad truth (and I want to leave you with this because it will depress you nicely until next week!) that the theatre is very cruel in the sense that it has to cast for exactly what is needed. Now what may be needed in a certain part is a very beautifully built, sexy girl who just has to walk across the stage to attract all the guys. That is precisely what is needed for that moment in the play; Eleanora Duse is not needed. It sometimes makes actors very unhappy to see somebody chosen for a part who has exactly what is wanted for the play but who has not studied and knows nothing about the Method, for example. What about Art, they say? Well, in permanent companies, such as we had in the Group Theatre you didn't always have just what was needed. You very often had to use the artistry of the actress and you built her up a little—but it is not the same thing!

Oh, well, see you next week.

MAY 27, 1957

THE METHOD AND "POETIC" THEATRE

I promised you that tonight I would take up the connection the Method might have with Poetic Theatre, Shakespeare, even musicals. First of all, let us try to arrive at some definition of theatre poetry. I am not one who believes it has to do only with the words, no matter how beautiful they may be. Not long ago an author sent me a play with very mundane situations, characters and ideas. He wanted, however, to make it into a poetic play and so the whole thing was written in a sort of fake Elizabethan verse. It all came out something like, "Egad! Prithee wilst thou go down to the delicatessen and fetch some pastrami?" I think that theatre poetry is a combining of all the stage arts—words and speech, thoughts and feelings, movement and gesture, décor (sets, lighting, costumes, props) and possibly music—all conspiring to evoke the same poetic concept at the same time. There is a mistaken conception that style in the theatre is something external only, a sort of elegant manner of posturing, plus speaking beautiful emptinesses, and that realism is deeply felt psychological truth with no attention to form at all. I think they are

123

both wrong. All art has form. Realism must have its form too or it descends into the slice-of-life naturalism that is no art at all. I feel, for example, that Gorki's *The Lower Depths*, although the situations and characters are from a very mean life, is written in the form of a beautiful mosaic with a very high poetic aspiration of feeling, a yearning for a better life.

Last week we examined the form of the realistic play; tonight let's take a look at the problems of poetic theatre. I went to the dictionary and looked up the definition of poetry. Again, Webster did not disappoint me. He said, "That form of literature which is characteristically free in its imaginative and emotional range but restricted by its acceptance of a form of expression imposing the conditions of musical beauty, and which, though not bound down to the representation and rational interpretation of that which has happened or may happen in real life, must achieve a kind of truth that is appropriate to the poet's conception and results from integrity of treatment affecting both the details and the fundamental principles." A wonderful book, the dictionary!

In poetry, one essential ingredient is the sense of imagery. Poets evolved a school which used imagism, as they called it, with which they created, achieved, conveyed, emotion or affection (see where "affective memory" comes from) not through concepts of things, but through things themselves. To give a quick example that comes to mind: Carl Sandburg, when he spoke of wedlock in a poem did not say that it is a state of matrimony, which is a concept, but said, "Wedlock is a padlock."

Now, an example of imagery and how it is created in

124

the theatre: In a play I directed called *My Heart's in the Highlands*, there was a moment where an old Shakespearean actor played a tune on a horn for the villagers, and they, in order to thank him, offered him gifts. The play was, to me, about the position of the artist in the world. That particular moment, I felt, meant that people are nourished by art, and I had the image of a plant flowering as it is being watered. How I executed that idea on the stage was, first, to have the old man high up on the porch playing his trumpet, with the people below. As he became more and more moved he started to quiver (this was justified by the actor's very real feeling, you understand) and he appeared to be using his trumpet like a watering can. The people standing around below were gradually attracted to the sound and in order to listen more comfortably, a couple of them knelt down on one knee, a little child was lifted up on somebody's shoulder (all very "true" elements, you see), and when this movement was completed, the crowd was formed roughly into the shape of a tree. Now each person also had concealed in his hand a nicely colored prop, a piece of vegetable or fruit or whatever. As they listened they slowly offered these things up to the old man. Each hand that came out, presumably from this tree, had one of these props in it. The actors were still doing something real (offering gifts), but it was gradually seeming to be a tree that was flowering. Then, as they listened to the music, they started to hum and sway, and the whole effect became like a tree swaying in a breeze. And at the very end of the piece, just because I couldn't resist it, the little child on the very top held up a gaily colored chicken.

It comes down to a matter of choice. Although what each actor did was real and could be justified, there were lots of real things they might have done that they didn't. They behaved in a certain, controlled way. It was not necessary for the people to walk up and hand the gifts to him, for example. All of those inessentials, real as they might be, were cut away so that I arrived at the image, the essence. It is very much like the analogy of a sculptor who comes to a stone and sees inside some image, some statue. To everyone else it looks like a rock, but because he is an artist, he sees something in there. So he starts chipping away his little pieces of stone. Now the important thing to remember is that the pieces of stone that he chips away are just as real as the piece that is left. It is all good stone but he just doesn't need those little chips; they are inessential to him. Finally, he arrives at the essence; or what his vision showed him in the first place.

So we begin to see that theatre poetry is concerned not only with poetic words but with a kind of unification of all the theatre arts, of which words are only one element. One could even do without them, and there has been theatre without words.

Now you might say, "That's the director's job you're talking about. Where does the actor come in?" Well, I think that the actor too, in addition to his precious element of emotion, must be able to use all the resources of theatre art—movement, voice, appreciation of music, etc. Without them he cannot execute the required result. I was once working on a poetic play in which an actress had to do a speech telling the story of her life. While this was unfolding I wanted to have a lone, high soprano off-stage wailing very softly. It was her heart crying as she spoke. But when we came to it, the actress turned to me and said, "Is *that* going to be going on while I'm acting?" Well, I was young then and out went the soprano wail; then something else went out of the production scheme; and then something else. Finally I went out. One of the actors told me later on, when the show was being re-directed by the producer, that when they were lighting out of town, the producer was heard to call up to the electrician, "Bring up the blue foots, Joe! All the poetry's gone out of this thing!"

Now we come to the problem of verse speaking or poetic speech. To hear the controversy about that you would think it had to be either "beautifully" spoken in a phony "English" accent but empty of feeling; or deeply, personally felt, and garbled in an equally phony "American" accent. I won't buy either. Fortunately I have been lucky enough in my life to have had it proven on the stage that it need not be one or the other. For example, I saw the great German actor, Basserman, play *Mephisto* in Goethe's *Faust*. Now that was certainly poetry, and yet it was a completely realized performance inside, with a great sense of truth, high humor, and yet completely respectful of all the problems of the language.

Well, we must give old Stanislavski his due again, because on this subject, in the book that no one reads (*Building a Character*), he says, "There are many actors who allow themselves to be carried away by the external form of poetry, its metre, and completely ignore the subtext and all the inner rhythm of living and feeling.

"They may be meticulous, even to the point of pedantry,

127

in their rendering of the metre. They may stress, with careful articulation, each rhyme, and scan a poem with mechanical precision. They are extremely fearful of any divergence from the mathematically exact rhythm. They are also afraid of pauses because they sense the vacuum of subtext. Actually the subtext is non-existent with them, they cannot really love a poem without knowing that which illumines it from within. All that is left is an empirical interest in rhythms and rhymes produced for their own sake, and hence a mechanical reading.

"These same actors have a similar attitude towards tempo. Having fixed this or that rate of speed they stick to it throughout a whole reading, never realizing that the tempo must go on living, vibrating, to a certain degree changing, but not remain frozen at the one rate of speed.

"There is little to choose between this attitude towards tempo, this lack of sensitiveness, and the soulless grinding out of a melody on a hand organ, or the tick of a metronome. Just compare this conception with that of a gifted conductor.

"For musicians of that sort an andante is not an inflexible andante, an allegro is not an absolute allegro. The first may at any time impinge on the second, or the second on the first. This life-giving oscillation does not exist in the mechanical tick of a metronome. In a good orchestra the tempi are constantly, almost imperceptibly, shifting and blending like the colors in a rainbow.

"All this applies to the theatre. We have directors and actors who are just mechanical craftsmen, and others who are splendid artists. The tempo of speech of the first is boring, monotonous, formal, whereas that of the second is
128

infinitely varied, lively and expressive. Need I stress the fact that actors who take a cut-and-dried attitude towards tempo-rhythm never can really handle verse forms?

"We are familiar with the other extreme of reading on the stage in which the verse is all but turned into prose.

"This often is the result of excessive, exaggerated, over-intensified attention to the subtextual content, out of all proportion to the verse. It becomes burdened down by psychotechnique in the pauses, involved and muddled psychology.

"All this produces a heavy-footed inner tempo-rhythm and a psychologically over-complex subtext which because of its involutions seeps into the verbal verse.

"A dramatic Wagnerian soprano with her rich, powerful voice is not chosen to sing the light, ethereal coloratura arias.

"In the same way one cannot weigh down the lightly rhyming verse of Griboyedov's play with an unnecessarily deep emotional subtext.

"This does not mean, of course, that verse cannot have deep emotional content. On the contrary. We all know that writers use the verse form when they want to convey edifying experiences or tragic emotions. Yet actors who overburden it with unduly ponderous subtextual content never really know how to handle poetry.

"There is a third type of actors who stand midway between the first two. They have an equal interest in the subtext with its inner tempo-rhythm and with the verbal verse text with its external tempo-rhythm, its sound forms, its measures and its definite outline."

I have done some work as an approach to this very end

result. I did it in opera where the kind of stiff, singing-actor is equal to the verse-actor who has no inner psychology to back himself up. The problem there is more aggravated because the mechanism of singing is even more involved than the problem of producing the spoken tones. I was glad to have the opportunity to try to solve this, since singing is a further step in the extension of ordinary speech into poetry.

What I did was to take a scene from the libretto and rehearse it first by speaking, instead of singing, the words without any attention to the musical form at all. I worked for all of the things you would work for if you were just doing a realistic play. I rehearsed for understanding of the characters, for connection between the people, for talking and listening, etc. Then I would have the actors go through the same section, with the piano playing the music, not singing but still talking. But now they had to fit their acting into the time space of the music—trying to keep their acting values as intact as possible. They naturally had to adjust their acting to the spatial demands of the form. In other words, if you had said before, "Hello, how are you?", and now found that you had two bars of music playing between the "Hello" and the "How are you?" you had to find out whether to continue the surprise of the "Hello" or start the desire to find out how they are during those two bars. You now had to extend your "intention," your thinking, through what ordinarily would be an unconscionably long pause, if the music were not playing. On the other hand, you may find that it is a very fast passage, and where before, without the music, you had been saying, in a languid drawl, "Gosh, I wish I didn't

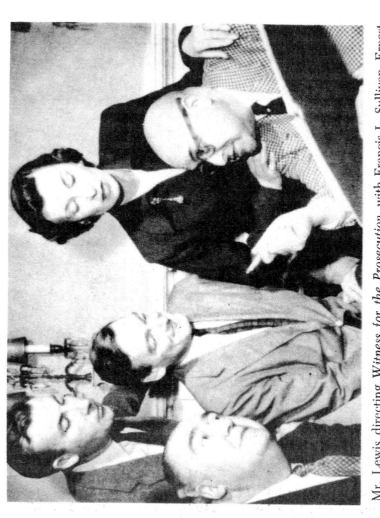

Mr. Lewis directing *Witness for the Prosecution*, with Francis L. Sullivan, Ernest Clark, Gene Lyons and Patricia Jessel.

have to leave this beautiful lecture hall . . ." the music now takes a quarter of the time you had been using. Whatever it is you had been working for in your acting, you now have to condense that amount of thinking, feeling, etc. into that lesser bit of space, or time. And you often find, if it is a good opera, and if the composer has some knowledge of theatre, that you are being forced into improving your acting, because he has given you tempi compatible with the emotional content of the scene. It is just like Shakespeare, who gives you the proper kind of words to say, if you play it right; he knows, through-having been an actor, where you can speak fully and at length, as well as where you should be too moved to be able to speak much, or at all.

The third step, after you have fitted your acting to the music timewise, is to add the singing. Since singing raises you to a point of general feeling by itself, you may lose some of the specifics you have worked for so far. But, you are compensated in another way since singing adds an emotional intensity to what you have already established, provided you can hang onto it. If you can, it prevents the terrible disaster of the usual opera acting: that the higher and louder you sing the more "noble" you feel—often the exact opposite of what you are supposed to be experiencing. If you have ever sung you know how good it feels to crack out that high C, and yet it might be the very moment when you are supposed to be murdering the fellow. So that "noble" sense of "beauty" that is given you by singing (or by speaking verse) is checked by having, in rehearsals, dinned into yourself the inner pattern of thought and feeling. In that way there is much less chance of falling into that kind of empty "nobility" that often goes with verse speaking or singing.

To give an example of how this all actually works out in practice: There was a moment in Marc Blitzstein's opera *Regina*, which was based on *The Little Foxes*, where *Regina's* husband, *Horace*, has just come home and the husband and wife confront each other for the first time in five months. (He has been away to a hospital after having had a heart attack.) *Regina* pushes the rest of the family offstage, turns and faces *Horace*, who is sitting down, and says, "Well." He answers, "Well?" and she sings, "Well, here we are. It's been a long time."

We worked on it as follows: I said to the singing-actress when we first went through the scene, "What you have to do here is to figure out the best way to deal with him. He's sick but you need action fast because your brothers are about to conclude a deal and you've got to get *Horace* in on it since you need him to get your share of the deal. You have to find out just what he thinks of you now, after all this time, so that you will know how to handle him." I told the singer playing *Horace* that he knows she is maneuvering something or she wouldn't have sent for him, and he is trying to find out what she wants. Now, we rehearsed that without music first. She looked at him and said, "Well," and laughed a little, trying to break the ice. *Horace* answered, "Well?", trying to figure out what she was up to, and she continued, "Well, here we are" etc. After we worked it out with the piano, we found the first "Well" was on a long low note in the orchestra which was held from the previous scene; and after *Horace's* "Well" there were four and a half

132

bars of music before *Regina* starts, "Well, here we are."
I kept *Horace* sitting in the chair after the first "Well,"
which was the held orchestra note. *Regina* just stood down
right studying him, while he just couldn't look at her. They
both held perfectly still, wondering about each other and
trying to figure out what to do next—that is what that long,
low, held note was. Then she broke away and I had her
cross behind him around the back of a couch while those
four bars were playing. During this movement she could
study him more openly and try *to figure out her next move,*
which was a continuation of her thinking. On the other
hand, *Horace* found it too embarrassing to look at her but,
as he mopped his face with his handkerchief, he tried *to
figure out what she was doing there behind him.* By the
time she came around front and faced him, she was ready
for "Well, here we are," and she could go on.

So you see that the problems given us by form are things
which can and must be solved in conjunction with the
inner problem. This is, I think, where the trouble has been
in the two points of view I keep talking about: That, although in the realistic form *what* one does and *why* one
does it are the two great questions you are continuously
answering in your rehearsal, the *how* you do it is, and
should be, present all the time. But in the poetic form the
how becomes a more important issue. The *what* and the
why must be solved too, but *how* they are executed, with
all the laws of art that are included in theatre poetry—
movement, tempo, spacing, architecture, décor, props, etc.
—must also be solved. For the director, all of these elements
must be taken into consideration; for the actor, his solving

of all of his external problems along with the internal ones must be accomplished. This goes for Shakespeare, musicals, and all forms of Lyric Theatre.

Now I want to give a couple of more examples from *My Heart's in the Highlands*. There was a moment in the play when the father, who was a poet, was revealed upstairs in his room trying to write a poem while his young son was playing on the street below. My idea was to show that creating a poem is as hard as any physical task that could possibly be set for a human being. As people in the throes of creation are kind of funny, I had the father in an odd position, kneeling on the table trying to write the poem. He was doing everything truthfully, really trying to think of the next rhyme, tearing up the paper when it didn't work, and so on; while the little boy playing down in the street was trying to stand on his head. This was creation on two different *levels* (literally and figuratively). Each time the father got to a place where he almost had a rhyme the boy almost stood on his head—and then fell at the second the father, above, failed. The idea, of course, was that one breaks one's neck writing a poem too. Finally, the father found the precious rhyme and the little boy did a whole series of happy somersaults.

There was also one moment when the old man in the play had to drink a glass of water; he had just walked five thousand miles and he was *very* thirsty. Now, if he is a "real-life" thinker, there is no way that an actor can drink a glass of water that will relieve his thirst after he has walked five thousand miles! But in a poetic play like this, one is able to drink the greatest drink in history. And we helped him in every way. First of all we gave him a huge pitcher which was in the shape of a beautiful woman, with the spout curved like her mouth. When the pitcher was handed to him he took it as if he was going to make love to it. As he put it to his lips and started to drink, music, accentuating the relief that comes from great satisfaction, started playing softly. Holding this beautiful pitcher to his lips to drink, he leaned back further and further, drinking and drinking, until he had drunk enough water to be satisfied after having walked five thousand miles, and the music crashed to a climax.

Now the actor, in a moment such as that, has to be cognizant of all these different problems: Let's start with the true sensory feeling, if you will. He was *really* thirsty —you can start with that. *But,* that was only the beginning! Because of that monumental thirst he could look at that much-needed pitcher and really make love to it. It wanted imagination to do that. But he also had to have an understanding of movement. He had to bend down low because the pitcher was a big pitcher with all the water in the world in it and was naturally very heavy. He started low and went up and back until he ended with a terrific backbend. It took the ability to move and balance. He also had to have a sense of timing because he had to start on the first note and finish as the music reached its funny climax. So you see, all of the arts of the theatre were employed there by the director, but they all were also being used by the actor. You cannot even tackle a problem such as this unless everything is prepared for it and unless the actor is able to understand and execute it all. That is the actor's problem in Poetic Theatre.

I would just like to conclude this subject by saying that

135

in all these talks I am constantly trying to keep my eye doubly-focused on the inside (**the** content) *and* the outside (the form).

Good night.

JUNE 3, 1957

REHEARSAL PROCEDURE—AND SUMMATION

For this, the last of the series, I walked
onto the stage to an especially gratifying
round of applause which prompted me to
say:

There's nothing people like more than a closing!

I would like to spend the first part of this evening's
talk in giving you a practical illustration of how to put
some of the ideas we've been talking about these past
seven weeks into rehearsal form. I will outline one possible rehearsal process which would, I feel, be a normal
way to arrive at the results of the full inside and the formed
outside that we have been discussing. I also recommend
this as something for you as actors to know, whether or
not you are engaged with directors who work this way;
because if you have some feeling about the orderliness
of procedure, it can help you to keep your own work
processes clear. Also, as I spoke earlier about teaching,
this is a good plan to keep in mind for workshop activities

139

too, whether one is doing a scene from a play or a whole play.

A character that you are going to play needs normal growth. How much time you have to prepare a part is not so important as the order in which you prepare it. You should not do things you are not yet ready for, such as the forcing of emotion in the early stages which does such violence to your insides; or the leaping (in the beginning) at elements of characterization which often leads you to the cliché rather than to the character.

The story is told of the pianist, Ossip Gabrilowitsch, who had been pestered by a young piano student to listen to her play. He had shaken her off a number of times but finally she appeared at his home one day and rang the bell. "Since she's come this far," he thought, "the least I can do is to let her play." So she went to the piano, sat down, and played a piece while he listened. When she finished he said, "Well now, that was very interesting. An odd piece though—what is it?"

"Why, it's Chopin," she answered.

"Chopin? That's very strange; I thought I knew all the piano works of Chopin, but I don't seem to recognize this one."

"Well," she said, "it may be the way I prepare my playing. I haven't yet finished work on this."

"What do you mean?" he asked, "How *do* you practice?"

"Well, the first thing I do when I get a piece is to learn all the notes. I practice them until I know them perfectly. Then I study the interpretation of the piece and add that into the notes. Then the last part, which I haven't gotten to yet on this piece, is to put in the sharps and flats!"

Now we are very often guilty of much the same sort of mistake. We are inclined to put our overcoat on the first day and then try, during the rest of the rehearsals, to get dressed underneath. Of course this may come from many things that we know about: such as the whole business of getting the part, of making an impression on the first day, and of not being thrown out after the probationary five days; but we can't take the time at an artistic discussion like this to go into all that!

For the first rehearsal, I always think it is a good plan to have one person read the play to the cast. I have followed that plan wherever feasible. Of course there are certain possible pitfalls in it: if the person reading is a very fine performer and forgets that the object of the reading is to convey the ideas of the play simply and straightforwardly, without any attempt to show how the parts should be played, it may lead to trouble later. One sometimes gets carried away in reading and some highly impressionable actors may have a tendency to imitate. I have found, however, that it is not too great a danger because there is an unconscious resistance in most actors, especially in good actors, to playing a part the way anyone else does. In fact, it very often happens that after you've knocked yourself out trying to hint how you would like a part played, they usually go to the other extreme—the direct opposite—before they come back to your hints. So the danger of imitation is not so great as some people would like you to believe.

I think the virtues of that way of beginning are many. First of all, if one gives a straightforward, clear reading of the play, the twelve, or however many, members of the

141

cast are all at least getting *one* impression of the play instead of the twelve they might get if each actor was reading his part the very first rehearsal, because naturally, each person has his own first impression. Beginnings are extremely important, and I think if you have one impression instead of twelve you are sure to get off to a better start. Also, the actors are much more apt to hear the entire play in a relaxed way if somebody reads it to them; more so than when they are tense about their first reading—and tense they usually are the first time. They wait for their particular speeches to come around and don't quite hear the rest of the play. Very often, in the third week you find the trouble is that some never really heard the play completely.

I find that the first rehearsal is usually strained for everybody and if it's over before the actors have worked, you are into your second rehearsal in a good, relaxed way.

The second rehearsal, naturally, consists of the actors reading their parts for the first time. This is a very important rehearsal. I think what the actor ought to avoid doing here is "trying to feel." If you have a scene where there seems to be some deep emotional content that you have to reach way out for, don't do it. It is not a good idea to *try* to feel when you're not yet prepared for it. Also, it is not a good idea to leap right off the bat at some characterization just because it seems to you to be indicated. A character may seem to be "a flighty girl" and so you might immediately start some characterization of "flightiness." It may turn out upon further examination that she's not so flighty after all, which means you've gotten off on the wrong foot. It is not a good idea to leap, without examination, at elements of characterization like this. However, I would like to say that one should not have any great terror of these pitfalls either. It is quite possible that the first time you read through, you might be moved by the play or by some situation that comes up in the play. If that were to happen naturally, I certainly would not knock myself out trying *not* to feel, which, in a sense, would be just as false as trying to feel. So too, some actors are able quickly to absorb an idea of a part and to deliver at once, without any effort at all, some correct element of characterization. It is just something they can do very easily. It would seem foolish to avoid doing it if it is obviously in the rôle and is going to be part of it eventually. Why knock yourself out not to do it just because it's the first reading? That too, it seems to me, would be false.

However, the things you should do in your first reading (because it is exploratory work and you are trying to find out what goes on) are *talk* and *listen*. By *talk* we don't mean just dribbling one word after another into your script; we mean a specific technical thing: to convey some idea to the partner you are addressing. Since it is only your second rehearsal it is perfectly true that you don't know all the ideas of the play yet. Some may leap out of the page at you and be perfectly clear, others may elude you, and some may even appear as the opposite of what they are eventually going to be. But at any rate, whether or not it is clear what the correct intention is at every moment, if you really talk to whomever you happen to be addressing, with whatever simple intention seems to be in the actual meaning of the lines, you are on pretty safe ground. It might be found later that when you say, "Give me a cigarette, Joe," (and that's all it seems to be at the moment you first read it), it is the very second when you decide to kill him. You discover that later and so it is eventually going to be quite a different reading from the first, which implies only that I, Bob, want a cigarette from you, Joe. But if at least that much is really done, it is something one can build on.

Listening! This is terribly important. One says this often and it is awfully hard to get it done right. There is that sense of rushing, of getting to the next cue; whereas actually, in the beginning, it is not important whether you come in right on the nose or not—you are not yet performing! But, when the other fellow is talking to you it certainly is a good idea to listen with the real desire to find out what the devil he's talking about. You will see that if you do not just listen to the prattle of his voice while waiting for your next cue, but really listen in order to find out what he means to say by his lines, you will be surprised that when you come back with your next little simple idea that it is already a bit more involved. It includes both things now—what he said and the little thing you intend—and you're in business. You'll be amazed at how quickly this develops if you will just do those two things, talking and listening, completely. Of course, it goes without saying that you should also listen to the whole play, whether it's your part or not, because very often there are important clues about your part in what others have to say about you.

In the next, the third, rehearsal, I think it's a good idea to read through once again and this time point out certain clues in the play—you can do it to yourself if the director doesn't, but the director should point them out to you—clues the author has put in the script. The director should stop periodically and point out from these clues the direction your part is going to take. Now it is the time for you to find out something specific about your part. After you've gone through it this way, having the sort of high-spots illuminated for you, the director should tell you something of the end product. In other words, he should give his production talk: what he is working towards, what his interpretation of the play is. Now that talk should not be too long! In the first place, if he talks too much about it he might get an odd feeling that he's accomplished it! Also, unless he has a very clear idea in his mind as to how he is going to execute all the production ideas, he'd better not state them too positively. What should be given in this short production talk and what you now ought to write down in your part is what the theme of the whole play is and what the theme of each part in the play is that is going to contribute to that main idea. There should also be some description of the particular style that this production is going to have, what you (collectively) are working toward, what your special production problems are—especially as regards the actors. Also, a word about how the play is going to be designed, costumed, and lighted at this time is very helpful. With this information given, you have a form into which you are slowly going to fit yourself. Now right after that you ought to read through the play once again and see how these production ideas of the inner form and the physical style really do inspire the actors to a greater understanding of their parts.

After that comes the next section of rehearsal, which takes a little longer and which I always find very fascinating. This consists of digging out and putting down, on the page opposite your speeches in your script, what you actually intend to convey by the lines of the author. I don't care by what term you call those thoughts, or intentions, but you should write them down in some definite way. You should know exactly where each section begins and ends. For example, on *this* specific line you first realize she may be lying to you and seven speeches further, on exactly *that* line, you know you are mistaken, that it couldn't be, not a nice girl like her, and a new intention starts. Through that whole section in between you *suspect everything she says of being untrue.* You ought to be able to mark your script in that way so that you can always keep the sections clear and know just where they begin and end. Incidentally, I love to give titles to whole passages in my director's script—like "The Thieves Fall Out" or something equally corny. The titles not only amuse me but they also give me an attitude toward that passage and help me to choose colorful intentions within it.

After that breakdown has been made you should then read through the play very carefully, trying to see how much of this inner form that the director has given out remains. He should also encourage the actors to act as much as possible while still in their chairs, or even getting up and going over to their partners in the scenes to play it. You are thus creating for yourself the *desire* to move, the need for the staging. If you *make* yourself get up and go, if you *make* yourself talk to him, if you *make* yourself do as much as you can—pat his hair, fix his tie

146

for example, in a love scene—awkward as it now is, it will make you so happy later when it is properly staged and you can do it right. All that has to be done then is to put you in a little better position and you can do it better. Otherwise the obstacles created by having done nothing until the point of staging comes, makes a whole problem with that tie—you should be half-way home by the time you come to actually doing it in the right positions. There are nothing but obstacles in the creation of a part. Each new stage of rehearsal creates obstacles. The next step (staging, the first time with scenery, or whatever) is always difficult and, when you take it, destroys something of what you have so carefully worked out. Therefore, anything the director can do to alleviate the torture of those obstacles will make the whole process of growing in the rôles that much more normal.

By now you are acting so much of it that you need to know exactly where you're going to be on stage. You are now ready for the director to give you the positions and the movements. It's a good idea in a realistic play to give the positions a bit generally at first in order to permit the actors to have a certain amount of freedom in playing; you put them in the general places where the scene is eventually going to be played. You don't have to have them exactly on a specific spot with the weight on the left foot and the right foot on the first rung of the ladder and so on —*yet* (we're coming to that!); but put them in the approximate area so they retain that desire to play the scenes they have built up. You give places to play and things to do which will fulfill what has been prepared so far. When the whole play has been blocked out that way, I always

147

like to have a kind of double process go on for the next couple of rehearsals. I take a scene or a section of it and have the actors involved do the scene in the chairs so that they get that wonderful connection again which they have lost a bit through having to get their positions. Then, as soon as they've got that connection back again, I let them get up at once and do the scene in the positions. I do each scene in the same way so that the final positions come out of what the scene is about.

During this section of rehearsal you should again be preparing yourself for the next obstacles looming around the corner: the scenery, costumes, lights, props, and all those things you feel ruin your acting after you've just gotten it set so fine. You should prepare the *desire* for them, too, so that you can't wait until they arrive; you should not dread that set rolling in, and that costume that's going to make you uncomfortable, and that prop that will prevent you from flinging your hands around. You should, with your imagination (the labor costs prevent you having the actual props), create for yourself all of the appurtenances of the stage. If you have to look out of a window, find out where it is going to be and really look out of the imaginary one. When the window finally is actually there, you'll be happy to see it if you have been using an imaginary one. If you have not been doing this, you are not apt to look out the real window and actually *see*. It is the same with every other element, too. Your costume, for example. If you are going to have certain clothes which will require you to behave in a certain way, you should either approximate or imagine them, or do a combination of both, so that when you finally get the nice costume from Brooks you will be pleased because you've been doing the right things without it and now you have a sense of completion. That protects you from walking around with your stomach sticking out for four weeks and then suddenly finding that your costume has uncomfortable tight trousers and that you must act now in these tight trousers. (In any modern play you have to!)

The same thing is true of props and even lighting effects. I've seen many actors suddenly thrown by being in what they felt was too much or too little light. There is no valid reason not to know what the lights will be like before you get to them, and then incorporate that knowledge in whatever it is you're working on in the scene—it is part of it!

Now we come to the last rehearsal process before we get to the run-throughs, which is the "smoothing out" of all the externals. By now let us say everyone is playing fine, but this fellow is in front of that one, or this grouping doesn't look right and you need to change a few positions, or somebody's voice has to be adjusted one way or another, or whatever. All the external problems can now be worked with nicely and smoothened out because you've got your form, inside and out, set. And if you, the actors, as well as the director, have done the proper preparation before, you will find it is possible for you to execute all sorts of things you could never have imagined possible earlier in rehearsal. You'll find, for example, you can be looking away from your sweetheart, instead of at her, at the moment you realize she doesn't love you, if for some reason you have to be looking that way. It can be a reason quite apart from anything you could have imagined. It could have to do with proposed lighting or scenery. Or let us say that the director suddenly feels it is more exciting for you not to be looking right at her at that moment. The point is you now know so much about it that the director can safely say, "Although you have previously been looking at her in this moment, I would like you now to play the moment looking away from her." And you can do it because you understand enough about it to realize the scene might be better for technical reasons that way, or more exciting, and to find a reason to do it like that. In other words, it is now possible for you, if you have prepared the earlier stages properly, to *justify* almost anything that is asked of you in the final staging.

And now we come to the run-throughs without sets or costumes. You go through without stopping and the director gives his notes at the end. I think it's a good idea, in the first few run-throughs, to give just the important notes, those having to do with big things. The fact that the boy walked past the girl accidentally and had to come back to say, "Hello, Joan," is not important, because the next time he's not going to go past her—you hope. Of course if he does it repeatedly, you have to point it out to him. But the chief thing is to give the important notes such as where the actor goes off from the main idea of the scene. If he can set himself right again on that you very often find the other things will correct themselves. Of course if they don't and there are certain little things still wrong after you've had several run-throughs, you can then fix them, even if they come down to one single letter of one word. Although it might be the tiniest detail, it could be very important, as I have pointed out before.

You then are ready for dress rehearsals with scenery, costumes and so on; and there's always some further adjustment on the part of the actor to all that. Then finally, the audience in New Haven, or wherever. The audience, too, makes other little changes. Certain things you were doing which you thought were perfectly clear are not clear to the public. In other things you find the audience is way ahead of you, etc.—and you fix and fix until the New York première.

Now the amount of time that should be spent on each one of these sections of rehearsal varies according to the problems of the particular play. There are some scripts that are extremely involved psychologically: the relationships of the characters, the probing into what the people mean by what they say, the emotional content of the scenes, etc. There may be few difficult problems of physical staging in a play of that type. Therefore, you naturally spend a larger proportion of your allotted rehearsal time —whether that be four weeks, two, or one—on the inner problems because you know you are going to accomplish the physical staging comparatively quickly. If, on the other hand, you are faced with a farce, let's say, which is fairly simple, psychologically speaking, but has intricate problems of movement and all sorts of effects, then, naturally, you use a lesser amount of time on the first sections of the rehearsal and get the play on its feet much sooner.

As a bonus for those of you who came to all eight lectures—how many did, by the way?—that's marvellous— well, I found something when I was studying the remarks of various directors on the problems of form and content in poetic plays, which bears on my talk of last week. It is so hilarious that I wanted you to hear it. It is a revealing example of how these problems were tackled in an actual production by two world-famous masters, and, as such, deserves our attention here tonight in the last lecture of this series. This remarkable document is a conversation in 1909 between Stanislavski and Gordon Craig. Craig, as you know, was invited to Moscow to design the Moscow Art Theatre production of *Hamlet*. Stanislavski had pinpointed the problem of poetic drama we have discussed by saying to the actors, "In *Hamlet* you are given great feeling to portray and great words to speak." He then got together with Craig, who was to be the designer, and discussed the approach to the play. Craig, of course, is the person that has had so much influence on modern directors, formulating, as he did, the whole idea of the unity of all the theatre arts in production. He himself had difficulty in putting many of his ideas to the test for one reason or another. At any rate, Stanislavski invited him to Russia to design *Hamlet* and to co-direct it, in a way, to get his ideas, since Craig was an Englishman and they were doing Shakespeare. This conversation is a comic example of what happens when the irresistible force of "content" meets the immovable object of "form." It was taken down verbatim by a fellow named Sulergitski who was a very reliable member of the Moscow Art Theatre. It refers to the third scene of the first act of *Hamlet*.

Craig: The scene takes place in *Polonius'* family. I should like this family to be different from anything that has preceded it. *Laertes* is basically nothing but a little *Polonius*.

Stanislavski: In what way should *Polonius'* family be different? It should not be likeable?

C: That's right. A fatuous, stupid family.

S: And *Ophelia?*

C: I am afraid so. She must be both stupid and lovely at the same time. That's the difficulty.

S: What do you mean—should she be a negative or a positive type?

C: She ought rather to be indefinite.

S: Aren't you afraid that if the audience, which is used to seeing *Ophelia* as an attractive person, saw her as stupid and unpleasant, it would say that the theatre has distorted her? Shouldn't it be done rather carefully?

C: Yes, I know.

S: It might be more tactful to make her attractive and pleasant generally on the stage, but to show her as stupid in some places. Would that do?

C: Yes, but I think that, like the whole family, particularly in this scene, she is a terrible nonentity. It's only when she is beginning to go mad that she gradually becomes more positive. All the advice that *Laertes* and his father give *Ophelia* shows their extraordinary pettiness and insignificance.

S: How should the audience see these people—through *Hamlet's* eyes, or its own? After all, *Hamlet* isn't on the stage in this scene.

C: Well, there's nothing in this scene which they need to see.

S: Won't the audience get muddled?

C: I don't think so. What's your opinion?

S: The Moscow audience likes to catch the director in a mistake, and it might seize upon this point.

C: That doesn't matter.

S: Yes, but we have seen from past attempts that on account of such incidents, the public forgot all that was worth while in the play, and used the opportunity to show its own erudition.

C: Yes, but you wouldn't wish to portray *Ophelia* as it's usually done—as a lovely, pure and noble person. Otherwise to my mind there would be no tragedy.

S: I haven't thought much about it. But as I am accustomed to think, and as our critic Belinski explained, *Ophelia* is a rather narrow, petit bourgeois character, but docile, with the ability to die, but without the ability to make any protest or to take any active steps. Nevertheless, Belinski considered her poetic.

C: Granted! But how can this critic consider *Ophelia* or *Desdemona* poetic if he knows *Cordelia?*

S: Yes, but Belinski, in comparing *Ophelia* and *Desdemona*, thinks that *Desdemona* might—

C: [*interrupting*] I think they are both rather stupid.

S: Then there is no tragedy.

C: Yes, she has generally very little connection with tragedy. I have no liking at all for *Ophelia*. The only ones I find attractive are *Cordelia* and *Imogen*.

S: And how does Shakespeare regard *Ophelia?*

C: In the same way as myself, I think.

S: I don't agree. If *Ophelia* had been merely a little fool, she would have degraded *Hamlet*.

C: She is only necessary to make the whole play a little more pathetic. That's all. The English critic M. S. Jameson
154

thinks she was silly from the start, from childhood. Perhaps she was frightened by a boy on a fence who made faces at her.

S: If *Hamlet* rejects a little fool it's not interesting, but if he is so up in the clouds as to renounce a pure and lovely girl—then it's a tragedy.

C: I don't see that. She is a small petty creature.

S: Then why did he love her?

C: He loved only his imagination, a woman of his imagination.

S: That will have to be explained in the intermissions.

C: *Hamlet's* mistake lies in the fact that he also imagined that *Rosencrantz* and *Guildenstern* were his friends.

S: But *Hamlet* never felt they were his friends. People tried to portray them this way on the stage, but it's quite wrong. He loved only *Horatio*.

C: *Hamlet's* mistake lies in the fact that he believes everyone to be as pure as himself. That is why he would like them to be his friends. For instance, he is terribly glad to see *Rosencrantz* and *Guildenstern*.

S: That does not appear from the text. *Horatio* he greets affectionately, but these two, on the contrary, coldly.

C: One of the most critical moments in the play is the appearance of *Rosencrantz* and *Guildenstern*. *Hamlet* wants to have them with him. They were good friends at school; that is why he sent for them, to have the chance of renewing the friendship.

S: But it wasn't *Hamlet* who sent for them, it was the *King*.

C: Yes, but they were brought up together.

S: Lots of people are brought up together! There's a

great difference between being brought up together and being friends.

C: Quite right. When they found out that *Hamlet* had not inherited the throne they went over to the *King*.

S: All these are details which, of course, are very important, but the chief, basic idea must be the collision of two mutually destructive principles—spirit versus matter. And our stage problem throughout the play is to find the right tone for the matter and the right tone for the spirit. What style should be adopted for each? Moreover this style should be apprehended not intellectually, but pictorially.

C: I see only one free man here. *Ophelia, Laertes* and *Polonius;* these are under the *King*'s influence, and *Ophelia,* besides, is under *Laertes*'.

S: Yes, these are features taken from life, entirely realistic, and the actors should try for them through characterization. The actress (*Ophelia*) should in this scene try for a tinge of meanness or pettiness. *Polonius* is an able, but low and despicable courtier, and his make-up is quite human, not over-emphasized, but his whole manner, his tone must reveal the base courtier in him. And he must be played absolutely realistically, to the point of banality.

C: Do you think so?

S: And these same people, in the presence of *Hamlet,* must turn into slight caricatures, not comic, but tragic caricatures. Then, perhaps, the public will understand your idea.

C: I shouldn't like a delete anything from Shakespeare, but there is so little in this scene that is worth emphasizing or in any way isolating. I like the Italians for their ability to glide through and deliver so easily those passages which contain nothing important. They do it so easily and pleasantly, as if tossing a ball. This relieves the public, does not tire it to no purpose, and for that reason the public can absorb the important passages when they come.

S: That is your own personal impression. I wouldn't have said so. This style of acting is nothing but the "stock company" system.

C: That's not quite correct. I have seen it in small companies where it was done quite consciously. It's a very subtle style of acting.

S: One Italian director who organized these stock companies told me why he did it. It's done because the leading man, who plays *Hamlet*, is not very gifted, so this method is used in order to single him out—it's common practice to hurry through all the passages where *Hamlet* is absent.

C: This is not any specific company. What I mean is that the ability to single out the essential with two or three strokes and to pass lightly what is relatively unimportant, is generally an attribute of Italian art, and that is their strong point not only in the art of the theatre but in painting, too.

S: That is the general Italian system.

C: Yes, but I think it can easily be acquired.

S: To do that, to make the scene go off easily and not have it draw too much attention to itself, there should be as little movement as possible. For that reason I should like to have everyone seated.

C: But the characters were already seated in the previous scene!

S: Don't forget that the hardest thing for the actor is to stand in the middle of an empty stage.

C: Yes, yes, I know! Can't you see *Ophelia* here, grimacing, in tears, with no particular inner sensations, standing on one spot, making no unnecessary gestures, not moving?

S: Do you know a single actress who could do that? Do you think Duse, for example, could do it?

C: [*roars*] Oh, Duse would fly across the whole stage here.

S: Then who could?

C: I think you have not one, but several people who would do it.

S: I know only one, but she doesn't like speaking either.

C: Who?

S: Isadora Duncan.

C: Oh no! She couldn't.

S: I have seen it. What you want from an actor is very interesting, but only a genius could do it.

C: Which of your actresses has the greatest sense of humour? I think Madame Lilina, so it seems to me. I think she might be able to manage this task. Nevertheless, I should very much like this to go off almost without movement. After all, there is no action here, only conversation.

S: And what is *Laertes* to do when he has to exit?

C: I think the whole scene takes place to the right of the audience. I should think that as the conversation nears the end, they all unnoticeably, smoothly, move to the exit from which they have come on to the stage. Shakespeare has no feelings or moods which should be read between the lines. He is too clear. In contemporary plays the mood is usually created not so much by the words themselves as by what lies between the lines, but in Shakespeare it is created primarily and entirely by the actual words.

158

S: Yes, but one must be able to make people listen to the words.

C: That is my intention in giving such simple settings, and I should like the movements to be simple and few in number.

S: Why do you think we make so many movements in Chekhov?

C: Because they derive from the play.

S: Yes, but strictly speaking in Chekhov there are no movements. We make the characters move only in order to make the public follow and listen.

C: Yes! yes!

S: And the most difficult thing is to place two actors and make them carry on a dialogue without moving. It immediately becomes theatrical. Not good theatrics, but banal, commonplace theatrics. What are we to do, in order to achieve not a vulgar but an artistic theatricality? In one of our productions, *The Drama of Life* (by Knut Hamsun), we found a means—

C: But here the words themselves are beautiful. The idea lies in the very words.

S: Don't forget, in the first place, that the words are in translation, and are, therefore, no longer as beautiful as in the original; and this is most important: To make people listen to beautiful words, they must be beautifully delivered. Furthermore, you want all the dramatis personae in this act to stand all the time. I should like to say that a seated position is richer in poses. There are very few possibilities when standing. If the actors are seated, they can alter their poses much more.

C: Yes, but I should like as little movement as possible

159

in the whole play. I should like them (the actors), without falling into strange poses in their search for simplicity, to understand that a performance of Shakespeare does not demand much variety in pose and movement. The meaning of Shakespeare is in his words. And it is possible to translate them into movements and acting only on condition that these poses and movements are as few as possible.

Now I want to take the last few minutes to sum up the points I have tried to make in these past weeks. First of all, I told you the reason for these talks was that a sense of confusion and bitterness surrounding this subject of the Method had grown to such great proportions, not only in the press and public but among the actors themselves, that I felt a public airing of the problems might lead to a clarifying of some of the confusion, or at least of our attitude toward the Method.

I said that the various opposing groups consisted first of the "true believers"—people who felt they had a monopolistic grasp on the deepest, truest meanings of the Master and that all other actors, all outsiders from the inner temple, were infidels. Then there was another group that I called "the angry knockers"—people who were just striking out and using the word Method as an epithet; and that very often their attitude seemed to have come from the feeling that somehow they were left out of something. A third group, the "giddy misconceivers," were people who had heard a little bit about the Method somewhere, maybe in a movie magazine, under a hair drier, or had attended one class somewhere, and were either Authorities or Knock-
160

ers but really didn't know what they were talking about. Then the last group were people who had a normal interest in all theatre techniques, of which Stanislavski's System was one. They were curious about it. They were interested in it because it is part of their profession. Or if they did know something about it, they would like to know more and have some point of view toward it—but toward *it* and not some rumor. And it was this last group that I was trying to expand with these meetings.

I then went on to say that the Stanislavski Method was *one* technique of acting, that there were others, and I mentioned a few. I tried to point out that all performing artists have some technique or other, whether or not they want to admit it or name it, and that it was simply a question of whether the technique they were employing was one which had, as its end (either avowed or unconscious) the self-exploitation of the actor, or the interpretation of a play and a part. And that technique was a means and not an end in itself, that it was a guide and not a fetish, that it was something that was there when, and if, you needed it to help you over the rough spots. There may be some people who don't need it at all, who have a natural sense of what is the right thing to do all the time. I don't think we ought to rely on that. I think that even if you feel yourself so blessed, it still is interesting for you to find out what the technique that you don't need is!

I then indicated that the particular technique we were discussing in these talks, the Stanislavski Method (that was under fire), was set down by this very human, working director in an attempt to isolate *what he felt good actors were doing when they were good.* And he had studied great actors and watched what they were doing when they were impressive. I then examined his attitude toward his own Method. Not that he needs defense from me; he was a great director for half a century. His reputation, aside from his System, is well-established over the world for his productions. But his attitude, from all the material that I could gather from the things he himself said, was a very fluid one. For over fifty years he was constantly changing and experimenting and improving. He had many different periods in his life, at least three major ones, in which he was constantly experimenting. Up to his death, he was looking for new ways of helping the actor to work. I said that it is a pity that followers of masters are often inclined to be more dogmatic than the masters themselves. While Stanislavski was very reluctant to put down his findings in any permanent form, hesitating for a long time, and only agreeing under great persuasion, there are others who will very quickly tell you exactly what those findings are.

Then I mentioned one circumstance which I think may be responsible for some of the misconceptions that have come down to the present day. That is the fact that, although the two volumes, *An Actor Prepares* and *Building a Character*, which embodied his entire system, were conceived together, they were published thirteen years apart. The first book came out in 1936 and the second in 1949. It is quite possible that a great deal of attention naturally was given to the first volume and sort of set in people's minds what the man meant before the second volume ever came out and showed the whole other side of the coin. I think if grumblers will take the trouble to read the second volume they will answer a lot of their own questions. They are continuously complaining about voice problems, speech, and mumbling. All this is very clearly spoken about in the second volume. I think that reading that second volume and getting Stanislavski's own views on these points will help a great deal to clear up a lot of confusion.

I then came to "truth" and asked whether the people who are always speaking of "living their part" are really living the part or really living themselves and adding the author's words to that life. And, while I came out "in favor of" truth, I also tried to point out that truth in art was a much larger concept than the simple, self-indulgent, comfortable feeling of the actor. That there are many elements that go into making a truthful moment in the theatre. That the truthful feeling of the actor was one part of it but not the whole truth, and that half-truths are just as untrue in art as they are in life. What, I asked, of the manner of expression, of the *use* of one's truth? Is it the truth of that part, is it the truth of that moment, is it the truth of that situation, is it the truth of that author, and is it the truth of that particular style of production? Those are all the truths that make up a certain moment. I said that if it is true only to you—if you "feel right in it" but every other element of art involved in it is wrong—then it is not true, artistically speaking. I felt it was wrong to condone the "indicated," unfortunately sometimes effective, kind of acting people indulge in where they are simply imitating feeling; but it was also wrong to call that kind of real, but personally-felt and inartistically expressed acting, truth. I think we ought to be able to reach out for a truth that is not only genuinely felt, but artistically controlled

163

and correctly used for the character, theme, circumstances, and chosen style of the author and the play at hand.

We then went on to discuss the point: actor or artist? Isn't it time we extended our interest to a sense of the whole theatre, rather than the world of acting technique alone? This would broaden our very attitude toward actual acting problems.

We spoke about the form of realistic theatre and I said that just because it was realistic, that did not mean it was formless. There is a definite realistic form that exists and I tried to point out what that form was—the successful scene-by-scene solving of the desires, wishes, intentions, whatever you want to call them, of each character in relation to the entire theme of the play. And that it was a form one could write down and keep and refer to, just as one could refer to a notation of a dance or to a musical score. I said that realism had its human problems, dealing as it did with the heart, mind, and will of actors, but that that is all the more reason why we should be interested in what will hold it to a form. In what I loosely called "the poetic theatre," which included Shakespeare, musicals, productions involving problems of style, there were still further and stricter questions of form to be observed. While in the realistic theatre one is concerned a great deal with *what* one is doing in a scene and *why* one is doing it, one should not be unmindful of *how* one expresses this "what" and "why;" and in the poetic theatre, while all should stem from what one is doing and why one is doing it, the whole business of *how* one expresses it takes on a much larger significance and a greater amount of controls.

164

In conclusion, I would like to say that it would be very nice if theatre people could give up, as wasteful of time and energy, the accusations of phoniness that are flung from one side to the other. The fear of being phony has become one of the phoniest things in the theatre. And I would like those who call people interested in the Stanislavski, or any other method, phony, to save their energy to study their own insides. Let them find out if, with their sole attention to line readings, speech, movement, posture, and all the various things they call "style," they are actually building on solid ground—on well-thought-out and truly experienced "insides." On the other hand, I would like those who call any attempt at theatricality phony, to study their own outsides and find out if their acting instrument (including speech, gesture, movement, appearance, stage charm, personality, sense of rhythm, etc.) is really developed. Is attention being paid to these aspects of the acting art with the same devotion that is given to squeezing out some feeling? And to whether or not this fine feeling that they might have is really being used to serve the particular artistic problem at hand?

I feel that all art must have form, that theatricality must grow out of, and be built on, real substance, and that truth need not be drab or limiting if it is clothed with a sense of form and nurtured by our imagination.

Thank you, and good night.